EMISSIONS AND YOUR LICENCE TO OPERATE

A Guide for assessing releases to the environment

Published by Institution of Chemical Engineers for The Secretariat of the Environmental Analysis Co-operative.

Applications for reproduction should be made to Institution of Chemical Engineers, Davis Building, 165-189 Railway Terrace, Rugby, CV21 3HQ, UK.

ISBN 0 85295 423 9

Representatives of the following companies, Government departments and other organisations contributed to the work of the Co-operative and to the publication of this document.

AEA Technology Plc
Assn. of British Pharmaceuticals Industries
BNFL
BOC Group
BP Chemicals
British Gas Transco
British Steel Strip Products
Cheshire County Council
Ciba Speciality Chemicals Plc
Contract Chemicals
Department of Trade and Industry
DoE Welsh Office
Environment Agency
Environment and Heritage Service N. Ireland
Environmental Services Association
Federation of Small Businesses
Fluor Daniel Ltd
Hewlett-Packard Limited
Hill Consultants Ltd
ICI C&P
ICI Group
IMI Refiners
Institute of Environmental Assessment
Institute of Terrestrial Ecology
Jacobs Engineering
Jaguar Cars Ltd

Kent County Council
Ministry of Agriculture, Fisheries and Food
National Power Plc
National Society for Clean Air (NSCA)
NETCEN
Non-Ferrous Alliance
Ove Arup and Partners
Phillips Petroleum Company UK Ltd
Pilkington Glass Ltd
Powergen
Rechem International
Rhône-Poulenc Ltd
RIVM
Royal Town Planning Institute
Scottish Environment Protection Agency
SGS Environment
Scotland and Northern Ireland Forum For Environmental Research (SNIFFER)
Soil Survey and Land Research Centre
Solutia UK Ltd
Thames Water Utilities Ltd
UK Steel Association (British Steel Gas)
Water Services Association
Welsh Office
WRc Plc
WS Atkins Environment
Zeneca

This guide is based on the report of Co-operative Work Groups on Ambient Quality, chaired by Glenn Campbell, and Triviality and Significance Releases, chaired by Roger Timmis. The Work Groups conducted their work between March 1997 and March 1998. It also includes a brief summary of the Co-operative's first publication "Released Substances and their Dispersion in the Environment", edited by John Lawrence.

Edited by Rodney Perriman.

Printed in the United Kingdom by Hobbs the Printers Limited, Totton, Hampshire.

CONTENTS

Chapter 4   Worked Example

Appendices

Appendices for Chapter 2 - Environmental quality criteria

Appendices for Chapter 3 - Environmental monitoring and ambient quality data

Index

Preface

This book is the third publication from the Environmental Analysis Co-operative (EAC). The EAC is an informal organisation of more than fifty industrial companies and trade associations, consultants, departments of central and local government, the Environment Agencies and the National Society for Clean Air. It came together in February 1995 with the aim of producing guidance for applicants seeking authorisation of processes under Integrated Pollution Control (IPC).

The first phase of its work was to develop guidance for compiling an inventory of releases from a process and estimating the resulting levels of released substances in the local environment. That guidance was published by HMSO (now The Stationary Office) in March 1996 under the title "Released Substances and their Dispersion in the Environment" (RSDE) (Ref. 1).

Since RSDE was published there has been continuing debate about techniques for assessing the environmental impacts of releases from industrial processes and how to compare the relative overall environmental impacts of alternative processes. Over the same period, developments in environmental legislation and environmental management systems have highlighted the need for companies to incorporate environmental considerations into all aspects of business management. There has been increasing awareness of the linkages between pollution control and Town & Country Planning and the need for more effective co-ordination between pollution regulation and land use planning.

The EAC's second publication was a guide to help plant managers incorporate environmental considerations into their project management procedures. It was published by IChemE in December 1998, under the title "Don't Forget the Environment – A guide for incorporating environmental assessment into your project", (Ref. 2).

The guidance in RSDE is limited to the first stage of environmental assessment, namely identifying releases and quantifying the resulting levels of contamination in the local environment. This stage is described in RSDE as *environmental analysis*. It does not address the question of how to decide whether the releases are acceptable. Experience with RSDE has also shown the need for more detailed guidance on some aspects of environmental analysis.

In March 1997 the EAC set up two working groups to consider what further guidance could be developed. This book is based on the recommendations of those working groups. It builds on the framework of environmental assessment that was developed in RSDE and provides a more structured approach for carrying out the environmental assessment of releases from processes requiring IPC authorisation.

While this guidance has been developed specifically for IPC, the principles and techniques recommended will be applicable for IPPC, which comes into force in the UK in October 1999. It is also applicable for preparing environmental assessments in support of planning applications under the Town & Country Planning Acts.

This guidance is published independently of the Environment Agency, although the Agency has been involved in its production as a member of the Co-operative. The techniques and approaches recommended will not guarantee a successful application; nor does the guidance over-ride any legal requirements or official guidance from the Agency or government.

Throughout this book all references to English legislation and the Environment Agency (for England & Wales) apply equally to corresponding legislation and regulatory agencies in Scotland and Northern Ireland.

References

1. Released Substances and their Dispersion in the Environment, published by HMSO, ISBN 0 11 702010.
2. Don't Forget the Environment – A guide for incorporating environmental assessment into your project, published by IChemE, ISBN 0 85295 422 0.

The aims of the Environmental Analysis Co-operative are:

- To develop practical guidance to help operators make effective assessments of the environmental effects of processes;
- To improve the quality of environmental assessments in support of regulatory permits;
- To encourage good environmental management practices.

In keeping with these aims and its ethos of pursuing them through consensus and pooling experience, the EAC welcomes comments on its publications. If you would like to comment on any aspect of this guide, please write to:

Publications
IChemE
165-189 Railway Terrace
Rugby
CV21 3HQ
UK

Introduction

Purpose

The purpose of this guidance is to help managers who are developing industrial projects that will require authorisation under the IPC provisions of the Environment Act 1990. The aim is to provide information, techniques and procedures that will enable them to compile the relevant information and make the required assessments as cost effectively as possible.

The book is written for managers and project leaders in industry who may not be environmental management specialists but who are developing plans for new or modified processes that require IPC authorisation. At best it should help them to compile and assess all the relevant information themselves. At the very least it will help them to specify and manage specialist environmental contract services and to prepare for discussions with regulating authorities.

Aside from legal compliance considerations, the aim of all EAC publications is to foster good environmental management practice. The approaches and techniques recommended in this book should help managers incorporate environmental considerations into their development plans and thereby improve the long-term sustainability of their business.

Scope and structure

Chapter 1 sets out the overall framework for environmental assessment in the context of an IPC application. It is based on the approach that was developed by the EAC in its first publication, "Released Substances and their Dispersion in the Environment" (RSDE) (Ref. 1). Chapters 2 and 3 provide new guidance on two aspects of environmental assessment which were not addressed in depth in RSDE.

Chapter 2 provides a structured approach for assessing the environmental significance of releases. This helps to focus resources for detailed assessment on the more significant releases and avoid unnecessary examination of trivial releases.

Chapter 3 provides guidance for assessing the existing quality of the environment that will be impacted by releases from a process. This is an essential element in determining the acceptability of a given release at a particular location.

Chapter 4 is a worked example to illustrate the use of the guidance from the previous chapters.

A glossary of terms is provided. Where these terms are used in the text they are printed in *italics*.

Limitations of the guidance

Environmental assessment is not an exact science. Estimates have to be made using very simplified representations of the environment. Much of the available information on environmental quality is based on limited and imprecise measurements or estimates. The recommendations in this book provide a structured approach for handling these uncertainties but careful and informed judgement is still needed at every stage.

The environmental effects of any industrial process are multi-faceted, with a range of greater or lesser effects in any of the media of air, water or land. It is not possible to reduce this complexity of effects to a single indicator of environmental impact. Indeed, any attempt to do so obscures the very information that people need for judging whether the combination of impacts is acceptable, or better or worse than the impacts of an alternative process. An underlying theme of this book is the importance of clearly displaying all the information that is used in environmental assessment and setting out, in a structured way, the procedures that have been followed to reach conclusions. By taking this approach the assessment is transparent and can be readily reviewed if any of the estimates, assumptions or criteria have to be changed.

Some of the recommended procedures make use of quantitative criteria to categorise environmental effects. The values proposed are based on a consensus view of EAC members as being appropriate for most situations. They should be used with discretion. The values should be adjusted if they are not considered appropriate for the local circumstances of a particular project. The important thing is to follow the structured procedure and to record the way it has been used.

Glossary

Definitions and explanations of terms - as they are used in this book

Ambient concentration (AC) is the existing concentration of a substance in air, water or soil at a given location in the absence of the process being considered.

Emission inventory is a list of all the substances and their quantities released from a process during normal operation. It also includes information about the location and condition of the releases that will be needed to estimate their dispersion and fate in the environment in the procedures for *environmental analysis* and *environmental assessment*

Environmental analysis is a procedure for identifying and quantifying the releases of substances from a process to air, water and land; predicting how those releases will disperse in the respective parts of the environment and calculating the resultant concentrations of the released substances in the environment.

Environmental assessment is a procedure for evaluating the impacts of released substances in the environment, usually by comparing the estimated concentrations of the released substances in the environment with appropriate *environmental quality criteria*

Environmental Quality Criterion (EQC) is the maximum concentration of a substance in the environment that is considered to be acceptable for safeguarding human health or other exposed species. The derivation and use of EQCs is explained in section 2.2.

Environmental Quality Standard (EQS) is an EQC value that is set as a statutory standard in national or international law. A prime consideration for the Environment Agency and other pollution control authorities, when regulating discharges, is to ensure that environmental contamination does not exceed EQS values. The authorities monitor environment quality against EQS limits and produce regular reports on the state of the environment.

Environmental thresholds are measures of environmental contamination, normalised with respect to the relevant environmental quality criteria, that are used to determine the degree of significance of a release. Their derivation and use is explained in section 2.4.

Mixing zone is the area of a water body around a discharge point which is permitted as the zone for diluting concentrations of released substances to below the relevant EQC value. Monitoring of water quality is done at the edge of the mixing zone.

Process contribution (PC) is the maximum concentration of a substance that occurs at a relevant target or place in the environment, as a result of its release from the process and subsequent dispersion.

Predicted environmental concentration (PEC) is the combination of the process contribution and ambient concentration (i.e. PEC = PC + AC).

Process footprint is the area of land or volume of the environment which is exposed to a detectable increase in concentration of a substance released from the process.

A *receptor* or *target* is anything in the environment that could be adversely affected by a released substance. It includes people, animal and plant life and man made structures (buildings, etc.). A *receptor* that is, or is likely to be, present in the local environment and is sensitive to a particular substance is usually used to determine the *environmental quality criterion (EQC)* for that substance, e.g. for common air pollutants the sensitive *receptor* is people and EQCs for most substances in air are based on their effects on human health.

Release concentration (RC) is the concentration of a substance in the total amount of a release from a process into the environment at the point of discharge, i.e. at the top of a chimney for a release to air; at the end of the discharge pipe for a release to water or in waste material deposited on land.

A *release situation* is a set of factors that characterise a release in terms of its source, amount, pathway, range, probable receptor(s) and relevant environmental quality criteria. Section 2.2 describes how to identify the release situations for a process.

Resolution of environmental quality data refers to the fineness of measured (or estimated) values of concentrations of substances in the environment. Measurements taken frequently over short time periods, such as every 15 minutes, give *high resolution* data; longer term measurements, such as monthly or annual means give *low resolution* data. The relevance of data resolution is explained in section 3.3.

A release is *significant* if it has some potential to cause harm in the receiving environment. The degree of harm that a released substance may cause will depend on the properties of the substance, the concentration of the substance in the environment and the nature of the receiving environment. Grades of significance are defined in section 2.4 by the terms: *trivial, marginal, medium significance* and *high significance*.

The *source-pathway-target* sequence, illustrated in Figure 1.3 is a useful framework for considering the environmental effects of a release. This involves examination of the point from which the substance is released into the environment (*source*), the route by which it disperses in the environment (*pathway*) and any sensitive receptors it may affect along the way (*targets*). The procedures for *environmental analysis* and *environmental assessment* are based on this framework.

A release is *trivial* if it that has no realistic potential to cause harm to the environment based on the type of substance, the amount released and the resulting concentration of the released substance in the environment.

Chapter 1   Environmental analysis and assessment for IPC applications

As stated in the Introduction, this chapter is based on RSDE. It summarises the more detailed guidance provided in RSDE, but it also modifies the original framework to take account of the new guidance that is now presented in Chapters 2 and 3.

1.1   IPC applications

All new processes, or significant changes to existing processes that are subject to the IPC provisions of the Environmental Protection Act 1990, have to be authorised by the Environment Agency before they start operating. An application for authorisation has to be made in the appropriate manner set out in the Regulations and official guidance. If you are not familiar with these requirements you should read "Integrated Pollution Control: a practical guide" (Ref 3).

Aside from the administrative and legal detail, the technical information in an IPC application has to cover the following aspects:

- **What are you proposing to do?** A description of the process with particular emphasis on all the equipment and control systems that you will use to minimise releases to the environment. This information must be in sufficient detail to show that the process will satisfy the requirements of BATNEEC for that type of process. The Environment Agency publishes a series of IPC guidance notes that describe the techniques and performance standards for each category of processes prescribed for IPC control. (Ref 4).

- **What will be released?** A list of all the releases from your process into the environment with the fullest possible descriptions of the types and quantities of the substances in emissions to air, discharges water and disposals to land. This is the emission inventory.
  The word *release* is used to mean all the substances rejected from the IPC process as wastes, whether emitted to air, discharged to water or deposited on land.

- **What will happen to the releases?** Estimates of the way the releases are expected to disperse in the environment and the amount and extent of contamination of the environment by the released substances. We call this step environmental analysis.

- **Will the releases be acceptable?** Estimates of the significance of the environmental contamination caused by the releases in relation to criteria for judging environmental quality. We call this step environmental assessment.

The primary objective of environmental analysis and assessment for an IPC application is to demonstrate that releases from the process would not cause "harm" in the environment. "Harm" in this context is defined in the Environmental Protection Act 1990 as "harm to the health of living organisms or other interference with the ecological systems of which they form part and, in the case of man, includes offence caused to any of his senses or harm to his property".

This chapter describes a structured approach for obtaining and presenting the information needed for identifying, analysing and assessing releases for an IPC application. For convenience and clarity we describe these steps as discrete procedures, but they are inter-dependant. You must be ready to anticipate the information needs of later steps in compiling the information for earlier steps and to reconsider early steps in the light of what is found later. For example, the amount of information about releases in the *emission inventory* will depend on the type of dispersion model you plan to use for *environmental analysis;* the level of detail you need from *environmental analysis* depends on the significance of the release in relation to the *environmental quality criteria* that will be used in *environmental assessment.*

The objective of this book is to provide a set of procedures that will help you deal with these complexities as simply and as cost-effectively as possible. The procedures are illustrated by a series of diagrams - Framework for Environmental Analysis and Assessment I to IV - to show how they link together to provide a coherent structure for compiling the information on environmental effects that is required for an IPC application. The first diagram in the series is Figure 1.1 showing the main stages described above.

Figure 1.1   The framework for environmental analysis and assessment - I

BASIC STAGES

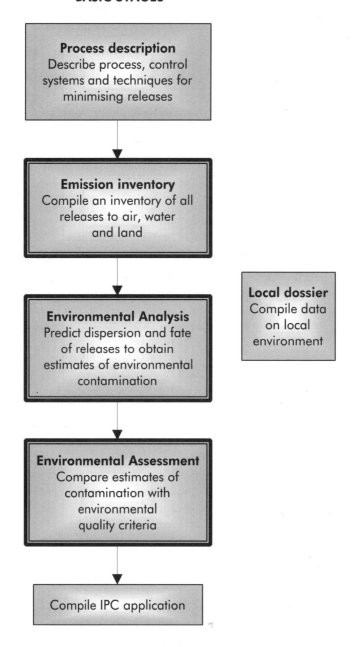

1.2   The framework for environmental analysis and assessment.

This section provides an overview of the stages shown in bold outline in Figure 1.1.

Emission inventory

The *emission inventory* is a comprehensive list of the releases from the process to the environment with information about their composition, amount and release conditions. This will include gases, vapours and particulate matter emitted from chimneys and vents, liquid waste discharged directly to water courses or to sewer and waste material for disposal on land. It should also include estimates of any fugitive releases from flanges and seals, dusts from stockpiles and any other releases that can be foreseen during normal operation and maintenance. Advice for compiling an emission inventory is given in section 1.3.

Environmental analysis

The purpose of this stage is to estimate the changes in the environment caused by the releases in the emission inventory. This involves:

- using some form of modelling to estimate how each release will disperse in the environment;
- understanding existing levels of contamination in the local environment;
- estimating the resulting levels of contamination due to the combination of the releases and any existing contamination.

Advice for carrying out environmental analysis is given in section 1.4.

Environmental assessment

The final stage in considering releases to the environment for an IPC application is to make a judgement of whether the resulting levels of contamination of air, water or land would be acceptable. This involves comparing the predicted contamination levels with relevant *environmental quality criteria* to assess whether the releases would cause any harmful effects on people or any other species that would be exposed to the contamination.

Advice for carrying out environmental assessment is given in section 1.5.

1.3   Compiling an emission inventory

Boundaries of the process

Before you start to compile the inventory be very clear about the boundaries of the process for which the IPC application is being made. Make sure there is no uncertainty about which activities and equipment are to be included. It is usually worthwhile making drawings to show this.

Accounting for all materials

The next step is to identify all the materials that enter the process - raw materials with their impurities, fuels, treatment chemicals, etc - and that leave the process - products, by-products, emissions to air, discharges to water or sewer and wastes for off-site treatment and disposal. Compile a mass balance to check that no inputs or outputs have been overlooked. For some processes a mass balance may be the best way to estimate releases, such as solvent losses, but in most cases design data will be the best basis. At this stage all releases should be identified and recorded, even if they seem benign or trivial.

Categories of releases

An IPC application is concerned with releases that are inherent in the normal operation of the process, that is those that are planned or foreseeable. The Guidance Notes published by the Environment Agency and the former HM Inspectorate of Pollution (Ref. 4) indicate which substances are most likely to be released from the various categories of prescribed processes, but all releases from your particular process should be identified. Releases that might occur as the result of operating errors, equipment failures or other accidents are not included in the emission inventory. It is convenient to categorise sources of releases from a process in the following way:

Normal releases. These are the releases of substances to air, to water or to land-based disposal that arise from the process running under normal operating conditions. They should be included in the *emission inventory*. They are likely to be specified with emission limits in an IPC authorisation or discharge consent.

Abnormal releases. These are other releases that may occur during operation of the process that are likely to exceed the normal release rates for a short time, e.g., discharges from safety control devices, such as pressure relief valves. The term may also be appropriate for other infrequent releases which are outside the *normal releases,* e.g. due to start-up and shut-down and maintenance. However if such releases are a regular feature of normal operations they should be included with the *normal releases*. An IPC authorisation may include conditions to minimise the risks of *abnormal releases*.

Fugitive emissions. These are mainly losses of gases or vapours to air from joints and glands in equipment handling volatile substances under pressure. Breathing losses from storage tanks are also classified as fugitive emissions. While each point source may be a tiny release, a complex plant may have hundreds of such sources resulting in a significant rate of release when the process is operating normally. An IPC authorisation may require an assessment of fugitive emissions and evidence that all reasonable measures are taken to minimise them.

Accidental releases. These are leaks or spills that may escape in uncontrolled ways into the environment. They are usually the result of equipment failure or operating errors. Airborne pollution and contaminated water run-off from fire-fighting are included in this category. Process design procedures should include hazard studies to ensure that risks of these events are minimised, including provision of containment systems. On plants handling large quantities of hazardous materials, emergency plans must be in place to deal with accidental releases.

Figure 1.2 shows the various ways that substances may be released from a process and those that are subject to IPC.

Figure 1.2 Releases to the environment from IPC processes

Product	Disposal to other processes	Normal releases				Abnormal releases Fugitive emissions, start-up, shut-down, maintenance	Accidental releases - Minor	Accidental releases - Major
	Landfill, incinerator or other external treatment	Emissions to air	Discharges to water	Discharges to sewer	Deposits to land	Flange and gland losses, tank breathing losses, releases and wastes during maintenance	Minor leaks and spills	Loss of containment, fires, etc.
Covered by product regulation	Record in application but controlled by regulation of those processes	Planned				Forseeable	Reported under IPC and elsewhere but not foreseen in an authorisation	
		Covered by IPC application and authorisation						

Where waste material is sent for disposal to a landfill site or an incinerator or to a recycling operation, it ceases to be subject to IPC regulation in its parent process and becomes subject to the regulation of the disposal or treatment process. However if that secondary process is closely linked with the IPC process on the same site it may be included in the IPC application. In any case the waste should be included in the *emission inventory*. Effluents to sewer should also be included.

Information in the *emission inventory*

Substances

As far as practicable, identify all the substances in releases as individual compounds. Where this is not practicable, for example a waterborne effluent containing a mix of reaction residues from a chemical synthesis, the material should be fully described and classified in terms of environmentally relevant characteristics, e.g. COD, TOC, pH, etc.

Quantities

As far as practicable all release streams should be quantified in terms of flow rates and concentrations of individual substances or other relevant characteristic. The basis for the estimate, e.g. design data, mass balance, etc. should be noted.

Remember that figures included in an IPC application form part of the eventual authorisation and may be specified as operating limits. It is therefore important that the quantities in the emission inventory are not average values but are typical of the highest release rates that are anticipated during normal operation of the process.

Release characteristics

This includes point of release (e.g. chimney height and location for airborne emissions, location of effluent pipe for water-borne discharges) and the physical characteristics of the releases, such as discharge temperature, efflux velocity, etc. The pattern of the release is also important, e.g. continuous or intermittent. The relevant characteristics are those that will be required for estimating dispersion at the *environmental analysis* stage.

Even at this early stage it is worth considering what *environmental quality criteria* will be used at the *environmental assessment* stage. This will ensure that the right sort of information is in the *emission inventory*, e.g., if the environmental effect of a release to air is to be assessed against an annual value of ground level concentration, the inventory must include all the information needed to run a dispersion model that can compute maximum ground level concentrations on that basis.

1.4   Environmental analysis

Dispersion in the environment

When substances are released into the environment from a vent to air or from a discharge pipe to water they are dispersed and diluted by the air or water flow. The resulting concentrations of substances in air or water at a measuring point depend on how much is released and how rapidly it disperses in the atmosphere or in the watercourse. Land contamination may result from deposition of airborne emissions or from wastes that are disposed of by spreading onto agricultural land. Whether a release leads to harmful effects depends on whether anything in the environment is exposed to harmful concentrations of the released substances. Figure 1.3 illustrates the dispersion of releases to air and to water.

Figure 1.3 Dispersion of releases in the environment

The behaviour of a release in the environment depends on the environment itself. The rate and pattern of dispersion of an emission to air depends on atmospheric conditions, such as wind speed and direction and the degree of turbulence in the atmosphere. It is also affected by the airflow over obstructions, such as buildings and hills. Dispersion of an effluent in water depends on river flow rates, tidal streams and salinity. The fate of substances in soil depends on soil type and land use. These factors will influence your choice of model for estimating dispersion. We recommend that you compile a dossier of the characteristics of the local environment that are needed for estimating the fate of releases and assessing their impacts. The **local dossier** should include, where relevant:

Meteorological data
Flow data for rivers
Tidal and salinity data for estuaries and coastal waters
Natural and built topography and surface features
Locations and nature of environmentally sensitive sites

A full analysis of the ultimate fate and effects of a released substance in the environment would involve complex studies of its degradation products and their uptake by a wide range of exposed plant and animal species. This level of analysis is not normally required for an IPC application. Instead we assess the significance of a release by comparing the resulting concentration of the released substance in air, water or soil with concentrations which have been assessed as "safe". We refer to these "safe" values as **environmental quality criteria** (or **environmental quality standards** if they are set as legal requirements).

Screening releases - trivial and significant releases

The emission inventory may include a large number of releases, ranging from substantial quantities to very small amounts. The potentially harmful effects of the substances may also range from severe to benign. To put it another way, the releases from a process may range from *highly significant* to *trivial*, in terms of their potential to cause harm in the environment. The procedure for *environmental analysis* includes a screening stage to identify the releases that may be regarded as *trivial*. Attention can then focus on more detailed analysis and assessment of the *significant releases*.

Chapter 2 describes a procedure for determining which releases are *trivial* and which are *significant*. It involves using simple dispersion methods to estimate environmental concentrations, then comparing those concentrations with environmental threshold criteria to put them on a scale of significance from trivial to high significance. Figure 1.4 shows how this procedure fits into and extends the basic framework diagram from Figure 1.1.

Figure 1.4   Framework for environmental analysis and assessment - II
(Screening releases for significance)

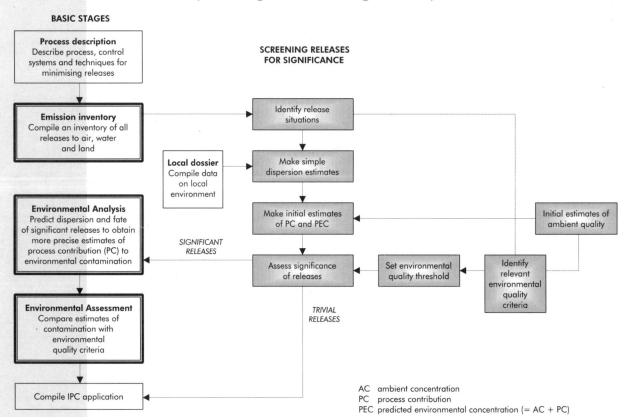

AC   ambient concentration
PC   process contribution
PEC predicted environmental concentration (= AC + PC)

Chapter 2 provides guidance for all the screening steps shown in Figure 1.4, including how to select and use simple dispersion methods and how to use *environmental threshold criteria* to rate the significance of releases. The screening procedure covers releases to air, water and land.

The outcome of the screening procedure is a list of releases that are *significant,* meaning that they should be examined more closely to obtain a more precise estimate of the contamination they will cause in the environment.

Modelling dispersion of significant releases

Having identified the *significant* releases, the next step is to decide what modelling technique is most appropriate for estimating concentrations of the released substances in the environment. The earlier EAC publication, "Released Substances and their Dispersion in the Environment" (RSDE) (Ref. 1), provides comprehensive advice in its Part B for selecting and using mathematical models for estimating the dispersion of emissions to air and discharges to watercourses. Appendices 2.4 (a) to (k) include all the reference sources quoted in RSDE.

The old adage of "garbage in - garbage out" is applicable to dispersion modelling. You must have a full understanding of the underlying principles and simplifications that are built into a model in order to obtain reliable results. If your organisation does not have that expertise in-house we strongly recommend that you use specialist services for modelling your most significant emissions.

The outcome of the detailed modelling of a *significant* release is an estimate of the concentration of the released substance in the receiving environment - air, water or soil. For emissions to air, the estimate is usually in terms of the maximum ground level concentration of the released substance. The value should be calculated on the same basis as the *environmental quality criteria* that will be used to assess the acceptability of the release. For example if the *EQC* is expressed as a one-hour maximum value, the model should be set up to calculate the maximum ground level concentration as a one hour value. For discharges to water the estimate is usually in terms of annual mean concentration at a defined monitoring point.

Ambient quality

The term *ambient quality*, in the context of an IPC application, means the concentrations of relevant substances that are already present in the environment in which a new process is to be located. These are present from other sources, such as other industrial processes, commercial and domestic activities, agriculture, traffic and natural sources. If environmental analysis is being carried out for an IPC application for a modification to an existing process, the ambient quality will include the environmental concentrations of substances produced by the existing process.

The main purpose of obtaining information about the quality of the local environment is that at the *environmental assessment* stage a judgement will be needed on whether the combination of the new process releases and the ambient quality is acceptable in comparison with the relevant *environmental quality criteria*. Ambient quality data may be needed at the screening stage (Chapter 2). If the concentration of the released substance is a small fraction of the ambient quality the release is not likely to be significant. Information on ambient environmental quality is not always readily accessible or complete or wholly applicable for a particular project. Detailed and comprehensive data on the existing concentrations in the local environment of all the substances released from a process is seldom available. It is usually necessary to make estimates based on extrapolations and comparisons with the limited data that is available for similar locations.

The quality of these estimates should be in proportion to the significance of the release. If a release is clearly *trivial* there is no need to spend time determining ambient quality, but for *significant* releases a reliable estimate of ambient quality must be made to check whether the combination of ambient quality and release contribution would exceed the *environmental quality criteria*.

Chapter 3 provides a structured approach for making best use of the available information on ambient environmental quality in the UK to estimate the ambient quality around a proposed IPC process. Figure 1.5 shows how this procedure fits into the framework for environmental analysis and assessment.

Figure 1.5 Framework for environmental analysis and assessment - III
(Ambient environmental quality)

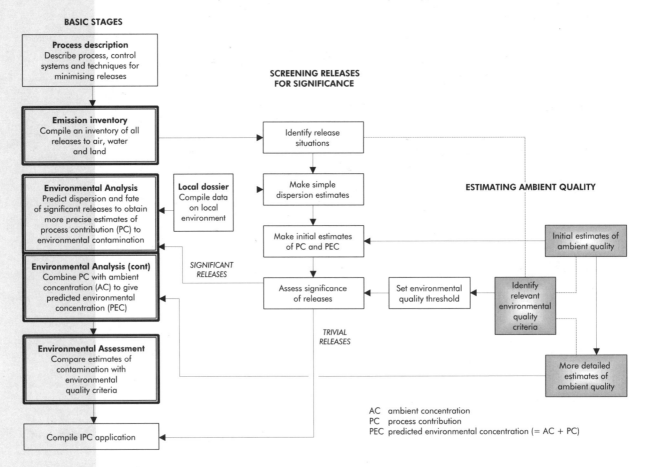

Predicted Environmental Concentrations

The final step in the *environmental analysis* stage is to combine the estimate of the *process contribution* (PC) of each significant release with the estimate of the *ambient concentration* (AC) for the same substance in the same environmental medium (air or water or soil as appropriate) to obtain your estimate of the *predicted environmental concentration* (PEC).

$$PC + AC = PEC$$

PEC can then be compared with the relevant *environmental quality criteria* (EQC) for that substance in the same medium. This is the last stage in examining the environmental effects of releases, namely *environmental assessment*.

1.5   Environmental assessment

The key requirements of IPC are:

- releases of <u>prescribed</u> substances shall be minimised by use of BATNEEC
- releases of <u>all</u> substances shall be controlled to avoid harm in the environment

As indicated in section 1.1, we use *environmental quality criteria* as the indicator of "harm" in an IPC application. Figure 1.6 completes the series of diagrams illustrating the framework for analysis and assessment with a thick line to indicate the comparison of PEC with EQC.

Figure 1.6   Framework for environmental analysis and assessment - IV
(Environmental assessment)

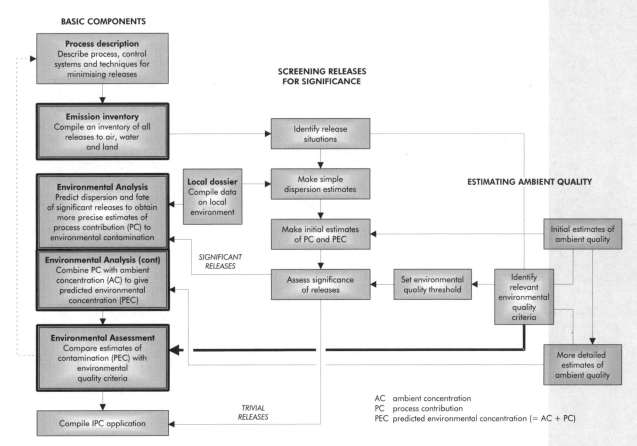

The first consideration of the environmental assessment stage is whether any PEC exceeds the relevant EQC. If that is the case the release is unlikely to be acceptable and the proposed process would not be authorised. The dotted line on the left hand side of Figure 1.6 indicates that the process design would then have to be changed to reduce or eliminate that release.

In practice this situation should never arise at this late stage. The screening procedure in Chapter 2 should give early warning of any release that is likely to give an unacceptably high level of environmental contamination.

It does not follow that every PEC that is less than the EQC would automatically be acceptable. In all its regulating activities the Environment Agency, in line with public policy, is seeking continual improvement in all aspects of the UK environment. EQCs are regarded as upper limits of acceptable contamination. A single release that produces a PEC approaching the EQC level would be closely scrutinised. The Environment Agency considers each IPC application on its merits and in relation to local conditions.

In Chapters 2 and 3, criteria of significance are given as guidance for determining the depth of analysis that is appropriate for a particular release. These criteria are based on the experience of members of the Environmental Analysis Co-operative. We consider they are a reasonable basis for assessing the acceptability of releases and the resulting contamination levels. At the very least they provide a starting point for discussions with the Environment Agency. The table in Figure 1.7, based on these criteria, gives an indication of the likely implications of a range of releases.between PEC levels from < 1% of EQC to 100% of EQC.

Figure 1.7 Acceptability of releases

PEC as % of EQC	Level of significance	Practical implications
< 1%	Trivial	Release likely to be acceptable. Good process control coupled with occasional monitoring of release.
1% - 10%	Marginal	Release likely to be acceptable in most situations. High level of process control and regular monitoring of release.
10% - 40%	Medium significance	Release probably acceptable but longer term improvement may be required. High level of process control and frequent monitoring of release, probably continuously.
40% - 100%	High significance	Acceptability of release will depend on local circumstances. High level of process control with continuous monitoring. Environmental monitoring likely to be required. Early improvement programme probably required.
> 100%		Release unacceptable in all but exceptional circumstances.

References

3. Integrated Pollution Control – a practical guide (DETR).
4. Chief Inspector's Guidance Notes, Series 1 and 2 (prepared by HMIP) and IPC Guidance Notes (prepared by the Environment Agency), available from Stationary Office bookshops and accredited agents.

Chapter 2 Assessing the significance of releases

2.1 Introduction

Chapter 1 has described the overall procedure for compiling and assessing the environmental effects of a process for an IPC application. Section 1.4 points out the need for identifying the releases that may be regarded as *trivial* so that attention can then focus on more detailed analysis and assessment of the *significant* releases.

A release may be regarded as *trivial* if it leads to a concentration in the environment that is extremely low in comparison to a concentration that could cause harmful effects. A release is *significant* if the resulting concentration in the environment is likely to approach a level that could cause harmful effects.

If a release is *trivial* there is no point in carrying out detailed analysis of the way it disperses in the environment because there is no chance of harmful concentrations occurring. But if a release is *significant* it is necessary to make the best possible estimates of its dispersion to ensure that nothing in the environment would be harmed by the release.

These rather obvious statements are not very helpful without answers to the following two questions:

- how can we show that a release is *trivial* without doing detailed dispersion analysis?
- what criteria can we use to show whether a concentration of a substance in the environment is harmful?

This chapter provides a procedure for classifying releases according to their potential for causing harm in the environment. The recommended approach is to make an initial assessment of environmental concentrations using very simple dispersion methods. These concentrations are then compared with a set of environmental threshold criteria to put them on a scale of significance from "trivial" to "high significance". Releases with very low potential to cause harm are classified as "trivial" and do not need further assessment. More detailed assessment can then concentrate on the more significant releases. By this means the time and cost of environmental analysis for an IPC application is kept in proportion to the potential of the process to cause harm in the environment.

For ease of reference Figure 2.1 is a copy of Figure 1.4, showing how this technique fits into the overall framework of environmental analysis and assessment.

Figure 2.1 Assessing the significance of releases for an IPC application

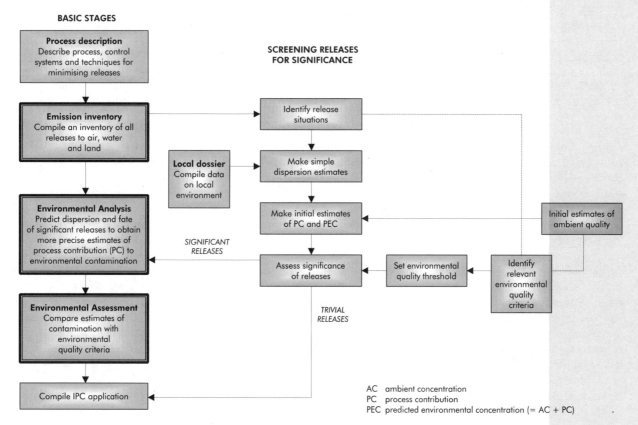

BASIC STAGES

Process description
Describe process, control systems and techniques for minimising releases

Emission inventory
Compile an inventory of all releases to air, water and land

Environmental Analysis
Predict dispersion and fate of significant releases to obtain more precise estimates of process contribution (PC) to environmental contamination

Environmental Assessment
Compare estimates of contamination with environmental quality criteria

Compile IPC application

SCREENING RELEASES FOR SIGNIFICANCE

Identify release situations

Local dossier
Compile data on local environment

Make simple dispersion estimates

Make initial estimates of PC and PEC

Assess significance of releases

Set environmental quality threshold

Identify relevant environmental quality criteria

Initial estimates of ambient quality

SIGNIFICANT RELEASES

TRIVIAL RELEASES

AC   ambient concentration
PC   process contribution
PEC predicted environmental concentration (= AC + PC)

Guidance for carrying out the shaded steps is set out in sections 2.2 - 2.4 of this chapter.

- Section 2.2 describes a procedure for identifying the releases that require initial dispersion estimates.
- Section 2.3 provides descriptions and references of methods for carrying out dispersion estimates using simple methods.
- Section 2.4 describes how the results of these simple dispersion estimates can be compared with environmental quality thresholds to assess the triviality or significance of each release.

The worked example in Chapter 4 illustrates the use of this guidance.

2.2   Release Situations

Factors to be considered

This section describes a procedure for identifying the combinations of releases and environmental situations that should be assessed for their significance. The prediction of whether a planned release could cause harm in the environment depends on the nature and amount of the substance, how and where it is released, the nature of the receiving environment and the presence of any sensitive receptors in that environment. All these factors should be considered when identifying the release situations that should be assessed.

The procedure uses the following factors to specify a release situation:

Type of release. All releases from the process should have been listed in the *emission inventory* together with information about the release characteristics. Figure 1.2 suggests three categories of release: *normal - abnormal - accidental.*

The guidance in this chapter is for assessing the significance of *normal* and foreseeable *abnormal* releases.

Release Point Conditions. This refers to the location of the release point (e.g. stack or vent location and height for discharges to air; position of effluent discharge outlet in a watercourse) and to the physical conditions at the discharge point (e.g. velocity, temperature, substance concentration, etc.).

Pollutants Released. These are all the substances that may be released from the process and have a potential to cause harm in the environment.

Quantities Released. This refers to the rate of release of substances from the release points. For a new process, the quantities will be derived from design calculations; for an existing process, emission measurements should be used as far as possible.

Time-scale. The length of time a substance is present in the environment at a given concentration is an important factor governing the effect it can have on receptors in the environment. Time-scales range from instantaneous (e.g. a few seconds due to a pressure relief valve venting) to long term (e.g. continuous release from a boiler chimney contributing to an increase in the annual average concentrations of oxides of sulphur and nitrogen around a site.)

Range affected. The locations that are affected by a release are determined by the above factors. For example, a small release of short duration may not be noticeable beyond the site boundary while a large continuous release from a tall chimney could produce detectable concentrations for a long distance downwind. Another important consideration under this factor is the physical characteristics of the receiving environment, e.g. would hills or large buildings affect the dispersion of air pollutants; would tidal flows affect dispersion of waterborne pollutants in estuaries and coastal waters. In Figure 2.2 we use the term "near field" for the immediate neighbourhood of the process, say within 1-2 Km, and "far field" for longer range effects.

Targets. For any particular release there may be several receptors that will be exposed to concentrations of the released substance(s) in the environment. It is necessary to identify those targets in the range affected that are most likely to be harmed by the released substance(s). For example, for an airborne release containing oxides of nitrogen in an urban area, the most sensitive target is the people living around the site who will be exposed to increased concentrations; for a water borne release containing traces of organic solvents the most sensitive target may be migrating sea trout. Relevant targets are normally in one of the categories of public health, sensitive animal species or sensitive plants. It is also important to consider whether particularly sensitive targets, such as hospitals, sites of special scientific interest (SSSIs) or downstream drinking water abstraction points, are likely to be affected by the release. Such targets may justify the use of more stringent EQCs in the assessment of significance.

Together, the above factors provide a complete description of a *release situation*. Figure 2.2 illustrates a tabular form of checklist for identifying the relevant factors for specifying the airborne release situations for a process.

Figure 2.2 Factors for specifying airborne release situations

Source			Pathway		Target	Environmental Quality Criterion	
Operational Conditions	Release Point/ Conditions	Pollutant Released	Time-Scale	Range	Targets	Type	Status

		Stack	NO$_X$	Continuous	At Fence	Local Community Health/ Nuisance	Short Term (acute effect)	Statutory	
	Normal		SO$_2$					Guide Value - human health	
			CO	Intermittent		Flora	Long Term (chronic effect)	Odour Threshold Value	
Start			PM$_{10}$		Near Field	Fauna			Finish
	Abnormal	Vents	VOCs				Odour (nuisance effect)	Guide Value - sensitive flora	
		Valves etc.	Metals	Instantaneous	Far Field			Fraction of OEL	

Note: Any pollutant transformation (e.g., conversion to less harmful substances by oxidation of hydrolosis in the atmosphere) is ignored at this stage. It may be a relevant factor at the later stage of more detailed assessment of releases which have been shown to be significant.

The right hand part of Figure 2.2 is used for identifying the appropriate *environmental quality criteria* for each release situation. It is set apart from the above factors because it can only be established after the other factors have been identified. This is explained in the next paragraph.

The term **Environmental Quality Criterion (EQC)** refers to the maximum concentration of a substance in the environment that is acceptable for safeguarding human health or other exposed species. EQCs may be derived in a number of ways, such as toxicological or dose response data or Occupational Exposure Levels (OELs) with added safety margins for substances in air and eco-toxicological data for substances in water. EQC concentration values for air and water are specified with a particular time scale or averaging time (e.g. annual, daily or hourly averages or maximum values or as percentiles). This combination of concentration and time is an indication of the exposure that could be tolerated without adverse effect by an exposed species. Below that exposure any effect on the species is not considered harmful. EQCs are generally based on the most sensitive species that is likely to be present in the environment. For substances in air, EQCs are mostly based on human health effects. For substances in water, EQCs are usually based on the most sensitive species in the aquatic food chain.

EQCs may be set as regulatory or advisory limits, such as:

- Mandatory limits e.g. EU Directive limit values and corresponding UK Regulations, where they are usually referred to as Environmental Quality Standards (EQS)
- National targets e.g. the objectives of the UK National Air Quality Strategy
- Guideline values e.g. those recommended by the World Health Organisation (WHO) for substances in air; advisory EQSs for substances in water that are accepted by DETR and the Environment Agencies
- Values based on dose-response relationships from toxicological or eco-toxicological testing.

Where people may be exposed to substances, usually from airborne emissions, you must also consider the likelihood of causing nuisance. Some substances, such as hydrogen sulphide and some volatile organic sulphur compounds, have offensive smells at concentrations well below levels that would be harmful to health. For these substances the EQC is based on the odour threshold concentration.

For each *release situation* the combination of factors will indicate the appropriate EQC to be used in the assessment of significance.   The main considerations are the hazardous properties of the released substance, the discharge conditions and the types of targets inside the range of the affected environment. The relevant EQC for a release situation should be the based on the harmful effect of the released substance on the most sensitive species in the receiving environment. For example, in the examples quoted under **Targets** above, the appropriate EQC for nitrogen dioxide in air would be an annual mean concentration of 200µg/m³, which is the current EU limit to safeguard public health; the appropriate EQC for an organic solvent, such as toluene, in a fresh watercourse would be a concentration of 50 µg/l as an annual average, which is the current UK advisory value based on toxicity to trout.

When you compile a release situation using these factors, it is advisable to use "worst case" conditions to provide extra assurance in the subsequent assessment of significance. For example, if the ammonia content of an effluent from a process runs at 15 mg/l for 90% of the time but there is variation in the process for 10% of the time, producing an effluent concentration of 20 mg/l, the assessment of significance should be based on the higher figure. This is a sensible precaution to allow for uncertainties in measurements and estimates and to provide a margin of safety for protecting the environment. For the same reasons, you should use dry weather flows for assessing discharges to watercourses.

Releases to air

The examples in Figures 2.3 and 2.4, apply the general checklist of Figure 2.2 to a combustion plant and a chemical plant respectively. The technique is to use the tabular form of checklist to link the factors that describe each release situation. If you display the information in this way you reduce the risk that any release situation will be overlooked.

Figure 2.3 Airborne release situations from combustion plant

The two examples below depict release situations for a small combustion plant. The first is for fuelling by natural gas, which is the normal fuel; the second is fuelled by heavy fuel oil which is a standby fuel. The site is on the edge of a medium sized town.

Normal operation - gas firing

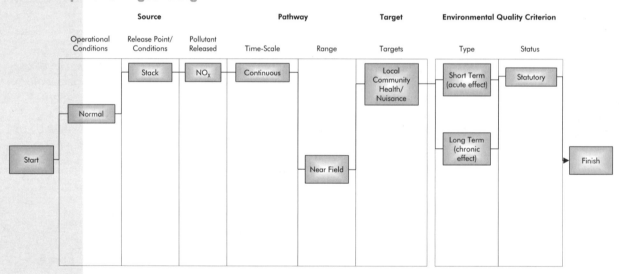

Notes
- Based on normal operation using natural gas as the fuel. Therefore only short term effects are considered.
- The process design indicates that NOx is the only pollutant emitted with potential to cause harm.
- The critical target is the local population.
- As gas is used for normal operation, the effect of NOx on the local population should be assessed over both long and short time-scales.

Summary Table

	Operational Mode	Pollutant	EQC
1	Normal (natural gas)	NOₓ (as NO₂ equivalent)	Short term acute - statutory
2	Normal (natural gas)	NOₓ (as NO₂ equivalent)	Long term chronic - statutory

Standby operation - oil firing

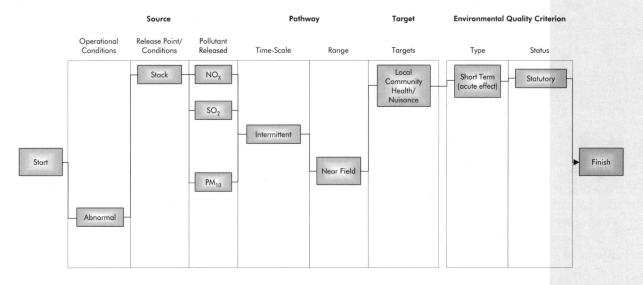

Notes
- The process is expected to operate on heavy fuel oil for up to 12 hours on 5-10 occasions per year. Therefore only short-term effects are considered.
- The emitted pollutants are NOx, SO_2 and particulates (PM_{10}).

Summary Table

	Operational Mode	Pollutant	EQC
3	Intermittent (heavy fuel oil)	NO_x (as NO_2 equivalent)	Short term acute - statutory
4	Intermittent (heavy fuel oil)	SO_2	Short term acute - statutory
5	Intermittent (heavy fuel oil)	PM_{10}	Short term acute - statutory

Figure 2.4 Example of an airborne release situation for a chemical plant

This example depicts a release situation for fugitive emissions from a chemical plant.

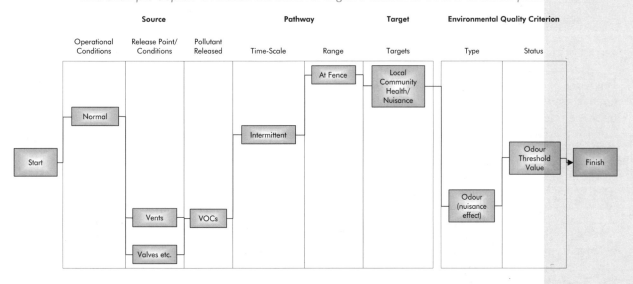

Notes
- During normal operation tiny quantities of butyl mercaptan are released from vents and valve seals.
- Due to the odorous nature of mercaptans, any effects will be felt in the immediate vicinity and targets will be the local community.
- Public perception of odour will be the significant threshold to consider.

Summary Table

	Operational Mode	Pollutant	EQC
1	Normal	Butylmercaptan	Odour Threshold

Appendix 2.3 (a) gives lists of current EQCs for substances in air.

Releases to Water

The general principles of the procedure described above for releases to air, apply for specifying release situations for discharges to water. However the factors need some modification to allow for different disposal routes for waterborne discharges - sewer, river, estuary, sea. There are also some specific terms used in connection with discharges to water. This leads to a rather different format for the general tabular checklist for specifying release situations for waterborne discharges. This is shown in Figure 2.5. The factors are explained in the following paragraphs.

Figure 2.5 Factors for specifying waterborne release situations

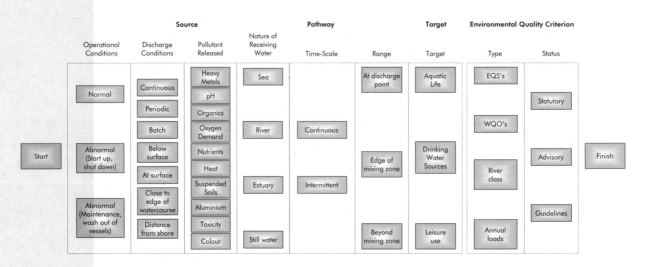

Note: Pollutant transformation (e.g. degradation, adsorption onto sediments) is ignored at this stage. It may be a relevant factor at the later stages of more detailed assessment of releases which have been shown to be significant.

Type of release

The types of releases described in section 1.3 are broadly applicable to releases to water. However, fugitive emissions are not normally a source of waterborne releases, in contrast to the situation for airborne releases where they may be significant. New processes should be designed to ensure that rain water drain systems are completely segregated from all areas where hazardous substances are handled. Operating procedures should minimise the risk of any contamination of rain water collection and drain systems.

Discharge Conditions

Whereas airborne wastes cannot normally be held before release, liquid effluents may be treated in batches from either continuous or batch manufacturing processes.

The direct effluent from a process may be discharged directly to sewer or to a watercourse, or treated on-site before discharge. This treatment may be specific for the effluent or it may take place in a treatment system handling effluent from several other processes. Such treatments range from full biological treatment to pH adjustment, settlement or filtration to remove suspended solids and dilution with other effluents. Where on-site treatment is carried out the condition of the treated effluent should be used in specifying relevant release situations.

The position of the discharge point may be an important factor in determining the way an effluent disperses in the receiving water, e.g. is the discharge underwater or at the surface; close to the edge of the watercourse or at a distance from shore? For releases to the sea or to an estuary, a major dilution effect may be produced by the buoyancy of "freshwater" effluent in saline water. Marine and estuarine discharges are normally on the seabed and a vertical dilution cone is produced.

Examples of Discharge Conditions

Nature of Receiving Water

Type	**Batch**	Single release of effluent, e.g. emptying a tank. Volume and frequency of discharge required.
	Continuous	Continuous flow of effluent, e.g. effluent discharged as a steady rate of release. Flow rate required.
	Periodic	Continuous, but from a process that operates for extended periods with interruptions, e.g. shut down at weekends or operates seasonally.
Location		Position in relation to receiving watercourse, e.g. surface or bottom discharge, shore line or off-shore, weather discharge via diffusers.

Unlike the atmosphere, which is usually regarded for this purpose as continuous and uniform in all directions above the single boundary of the ground, water courses have boundaries and characteristic flow patterns that constrain the dispersion of an effluent.

Again, unlike the atmosphere, which is usually regarded as an inert medium for the purposes of assessing the dispersion and fate of emissions, the nature of a receiving water may be an important factor in determining the environmental effect of an effluent, (e.g. acidic discharges are neutralised by the alkalinity of seawater; a rapidly flowing river with high dissolved oxygen will counteract the effects of BOD in an effluent better than a slow moving river with naturally low dissolved oxygen.)

Examples of Types of Receiving Water

Sea	Tidal effects help dispersion, but wind and tide may also bring material close to shore.
Estuary	A continuous discharge will be in still water for part of the tidal cycle and will travel upstream for part of the tidal cycle. A batch discharge may be arranged for release on ebb tide only.
River	Minimum (dry weather) flow rate required for conservative release situations.
Still Water	e.g. canal, lake.
Sewer	Many industrial effluents are discharged to sewer for treatment by the local Water Company in sewage treatment plants that handle a mix of domestic sewage and trade effluents. Limits on the quantity and properties of a trade effluent to sewer will be specified by the Water Company. The Water Company is responsible (to the Environment Agency) for the quality of the final effluent from the sewage treatment plant. However, it is good environmental management practice for the industrial discharger to understand the potential effects of his discharge on the performance of the sewage works and on the receiving water, particularly if his effluent contains substances that are not degraded by the sewage treatment process or could upset the treatment process. If the Water Company has difficulty meeting its discharge consent it will "look up the pipe" to find the trade effluent that is causing the problem.

Process effluents often contain a large number of substances. Full chemical analysis is not always practicable. However, if the effluent is known to contain specific hazardous substances their concentrations and release rates should be measured. Substances which are on UK or EC lists of hazardous substances (see Appendix 2.3(b)) should always be assessed.

Otherwise effluents are characterised by properties of the total effluent which are related to the effects the effluent will have on the receiving watercourse. Such parameters are: BOD, COD, suspended solids, colour, pH, toxicity and temperature.

Time-Scale

Environmental quality standards for substances in water are generally stated as annual average concentrations or as annual average concentration with a maximum allowable concentration (MAC). MAC values may be used to assess the significance of short-term discharges (lasting a few minutes) and annual average values should be used to assess the significance of continuous discharges or regular intermittent discharges.

Range affected

Unlike releases to air, where the height and distance of the release point usually provides considerable dilution before any potential target in the environment is exposed, aquatic life is exposed to the full concentrations of substances in a water borne effluent at the end of the discharge pipe. Because it is generally not practicable to treat or pre-dilute effluents to achieve safe concentrations at the point of discharge, there will be a volume of receiving water, called the *mixing zone*, around the point of discharge, which will be contaminated to levels above the environmental quality criteria. The size and boundaries of the mixing zone will be set by the Environment Agency. It will be site specific to provide adequate protection for aquatic life in the watercourse, e.g. to allow a sufficiently wide and relatively uncontaminated expanse of water to provide safe passage for fish around an effluent discharge. Outside the defined mixing zone, water quality should meet all the relevant environmental quality criteria.

This means that a discharge into a slow moving and narrow receiving watercourse may have to meet much lower concentration limits of harmful substances than a similar effluent discharged into a more turbulent or larger water course.

Environmental Quality Criteria

EQCs for substances in water are generally derived from measurement of the toxicity of the substance to species in the aquatic food chain, ranging from daphnia to trout. The appropriate criteria for a specific site will depend on the nature of the receiving water and any water quality objectives that have been set. Site specific guidance should be obtained from the local office of the Environment Agency.

Statutory environmental quality standards (EQSs) have been set under EU and UK legislation for a number of substances which are particularly harmful to the aquatic environment because they are toxic, persistent and bio-accumulative. Appendix 2.3(c) gives the current lists of substances with statutory EQSs.

For other substances which commonly occur in trade effluents, advisory EQSs have been agreed by DETR and the Environment Agencies. These are also shown in Appendix 2.3(c) and may be used as EQCs to assess the significance of a discharge

The Environment Agency is carrying out pilot studies to assess the feasibility of using whole effluent toxicity (as opposed to concentrations of individual toxic substances) as a pollution control indicator. This work could lead to new criteria for assessing the significance of discharges in the future.

Examples of Release Situations for discharges to water

Figures 2.6 and 2.7 illustrate how the general checklist of Figure 2.5 can be used to identify release situations for particular processes.

Figure 2.6 Example of a waterborne release situation for a metal recovery process

This depicts a continuous metal purification process, where a specific metal is being extracted from a solution containing impurities of other metals.

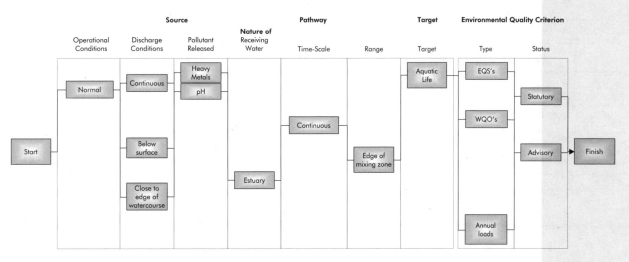

Notes

- The effluent containing the impurities is discharged to an estuary.
- The main pollutants are heavy metals and acidity (pH).
- Metals may cause a chronic effect in the estuary due to bioaccumulation.
- Consideration should be given to both short term and long term environmental quality criteria e.g. EQSs or WQOs and annual loads.

Summary Table

	Operational Mode	Pollutant	EQC
1	Normal	Heavy Metals	EQSs and annual loads for each metal
2	Normal	Acidity (pH)	WQOs

Figure 2.7 Example of a waterborne release situation for an organic chemical process

This example depicts a fine organic chemical plant that produces batches of chemicals to order. A different product is manufactured every 2-3 days and the production vessels are cleaned out between product changes. Effluent is treated on site before discharge to a river.

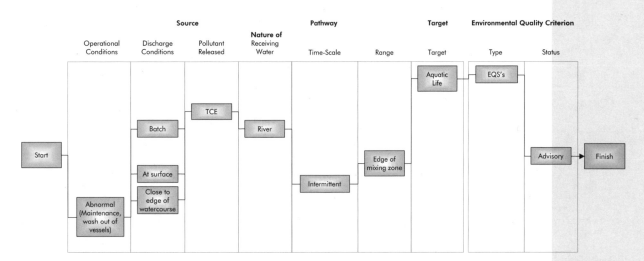

Notes

- The effluent is discharged into a river.
- The pollutant of concern is trichloroethylene.
- Assessment should be against peak concentration in river water.

Summary Table

	Operational Mode	Pollutant	EQC
1	Normal	Trichloroethylene	Advisory EQS

Releases to land

There are two types of release situations (apart from waste disposal to landfill sites) which lead to dispersal of released substances onto land. These are:

- deposition from airborne releases, such a particulates containing heavy metals e.g. from lead and zinc smelting; copper refining, metal recovery processes;
- direct spreading of wastes onto agricultural land as a means of waste disposal with soil conditioning benefits, e.g. sewage sludge spreading, disposal of some food industry wastes.

Airborne deposition

The general format of the tabular checklist in Figure 2.2 can be used for identifying release situations that are likely to cause airborne deposition of harmful substances on to land. For this environmental effect, the relevant EQC are limits of the acceptable concentrations of substances in surface soil. Such criteria depend on the intended use of the land exposed to the deposition. Appendix 2.3 (d) gives a list of current EQCs for substances in soils.

Direct spreading of wastes onto land

The release situations will be self evident since they are planned transportation of a waste stream to specified disposal sites. The EQCs in Appendix 2.3 (d) can also be used for this type of release situation.

Figure 2.8 illustrates the use of factors for specifying release situations involving deposition onto land by either of the above routes.

Figure 2.8 Factors for specifying release situations causing deposition to land

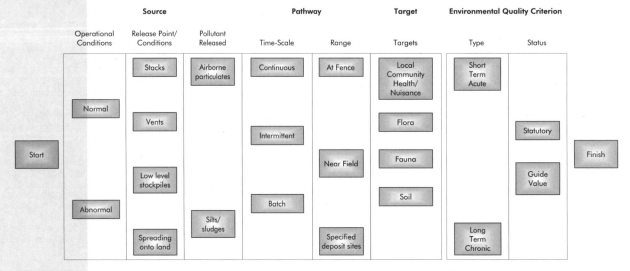

Application in practice

The techniques described in this section for identifying all the release situations that should be assessed must be used carefully to avoid generating an unreasonably and unnecessarily large number of situations for assessment. The following points should be kept in mind:

- The main purpose of IPC regulation is to prevent environmental harm from expected releases. The main effort should be directed to ensuring that all NORMAL RELEASES are identified for assessment.

- If the most pessimistic situations (i.e. those that would clearly have the greatest impacts) are assessed first and shown to be acceptable, then detailed consideration of less impacting situations may be unnecessary.

- Release situations identified for ABNORMAL RELEASES should be based on formal hazard study and risk assessment procedures and thereby limited to predictable situations that are inherent in the design of the process.

- ACCIDENTAL RELEASES should not be considered as release situations in this context. Hazard study and risk assessment procedures should be used to identify risk control measures that will reduce the risks of accidental releases to acceptable limits.

2.3   Methods for estimating dispersion of releases

Introduction

This section provides guidance for selecting and using simple methods for making initial estimates of the dispersion of released substances in the environment.

The term "simple methods" is used for quick and relatively easy techniques for making an initial estimate of the concentration of a released substance in the environment. The estimates will be approximate but this is usually sufficient for assessing whether the release is significant and warrants more sophisticated analysis using detailed mathematical models.

The simple methods we have selected are derived from modelling results for typical situations. Simple formulae or look-up charts enable you to make initial dispersion estimates without the need for detailed knowledge of the flow patterns and other dispersion characteristics in the local environment.

This section provides information about the reference sources for the methods we recommend so that you can justify, in your IPC application, the simple method(s) you have used to screen the releases from your process. More detailed information for each reference source is provided in Appendices 2.3 (a) - (j).

In the following sections we use a series of figures to illustrate the simple methods. Each figure uses schematic diagrams of the dispersion processes in the environment to show how the complex diluting mechanisms are reduced to very basic forms for the purposes of modelling. The codes (RS 1, RS 2 etc) for the reference sources are included in the figures.

The reference sources quoted in the figures are by no means exhaustive. Appendix 2.3 (k) provides a more comprehensive list. Appendix 2.3 (l) gives references for computer models that can be used for more advanced air and water dispersion modelling.

Releases to air

Dispersion of airborne releases

Figure 2.9 illustrates dispersion of a gaseous plume.

Figure 2.9 Gaseous Plumes

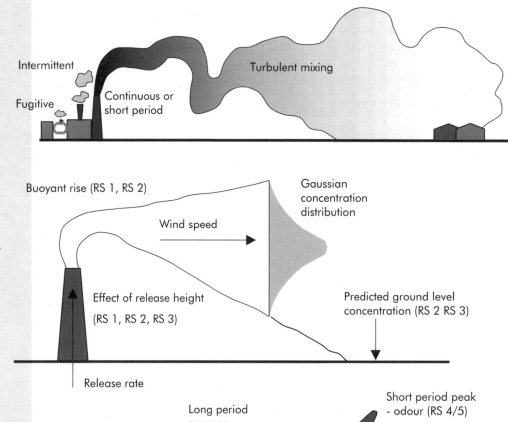

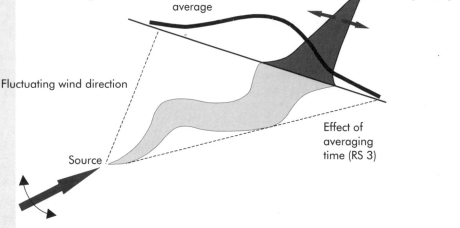

Note: RS 1, RS 2, etc are the References Sources we have used to derive the quick methods for estimating airborne dispersion.

The upper diagram in Figure 2.9 shows a vertical section along a plume from a continuous release. This illustrates the typical pathway and dispersion of a gas during its progress from the point of emission to the receptor - houses in this instance. The middle diagram shows the distribution of concentration of gas over the depth of a plume at a short distance downwind from the source. This type of distribution is known as a statistically 'normal' or 'Gaussian' profile. Such a distribution pattern can be expressed in mathematical terms. Simple models of gas dispersion usually assume that both the horizontal and vertical distributions are Gaussian in form.

The concentration of gas at ground level, which is usually the parameter of most interest, is influenced by the 'effective' stack height. This is the actual height of the stack plus any additional rise due to the exit velocity and buoyancy of warm flue gases.

The lower diagram of Figure 2.9 illustrates the wavering of a plume produced by fluctuations in the direction of the wind. If gas concentrations were measured at positions along a transverse line downwind from the source, then the width and peak concentration of the distribution would depend on the averaging period selected for the sampling of the gas. Multiple samples taken downwind for short periods, such as a few minutes, will show a mix of high and low results. Samples taken over longer periods, such as a few hours, will show more uniform results. Simple formulae are available to transform results from one averaging time to another.

Simple methods for estimating airborne dispersion

(i)   Reference source RS 1 - *Technical Guidance Note (Dispersion) D1 - Guidelines on Discharge Stack Heights for Polluting Emissions,* published by HMSO for HMIP (1993)

This document provides a formula and a look-up chart to relate release rate and vent height to maximum ground level concentration, based on average UK weather conditions. It also includes simple methods for estimating plume rise due to thermal buoyancy and efflux velocity. The formulae and chart can be used for either determining the required chimney height for a release or for estimating the maximum ground level concentration of a release from an existing chimney.

The main features of the method, with the formulae and look-up chart, are given in Appendix 2.3 (a)

(ii)   Reference source RS 2 - *Workbook of Atmospheric Dispersion Estimates: An introduction to dispersion modelling,* by D.B. Turner, published by Lewis (1991)

This workbook is an introduction to atmospheric dispersion modelling with example calculations. It provides a formula relating maximum ground level concentration to release rate, effective stack height and wind speed and a look-up chart relating maximum ground level concentration and distance from release point for a range of stack heights and weather conditions. Weather conditions are described in terms of Pasquill stability categories.

The main features of the workbook, with the formulae and look-up chart, are given in Appendix 2.3 (b)

(iii) Reference source RS 3 - *A model for short and medium range dispersion of radio-nuclides released to the atmosphere,* by R.H. Clarke, published by NRPB (1979)

Although the title refers to radioactive substances, the model is equally applicable to the dispersion of any airborne gaseous substances or very fine particulates. Look-up charts relate ground level concentrations to release patterns and stack heights for a variety of weather conditions. Information is given on the frequency of different weather conditions (as Pasquill stability categories) across the UK.

The main features of the model, known as NRPB-R91, are given in Appendix 2.3(c), with examples of the look-up charts and their use.

Special considerations for releases of odorous substances

Some volatile substances produce offensive smells at concentrations well below levels that would cause harm to human health. Examples are low molecular weight organic sulphur and nitrogen compounds and complex mixtures of these and other substances from various animal product processes.

The strength of the odour of a substance in air is expressed in terms of the Odour Threshold (OT) concentration. This is the lowest concentration at which the smell is detectable by 50% of a group of people selected for their keen sense of smell. Research into the public's response to odours indicates that an airborne release is likely to be regarded as a nuisance when its concentration in air is greater than 5 x OT. This concentration is referred to as the Odour Nuisance Threshold (ONT).

A release from a vent which has no substance (or mix of substances) in a concentration greater than the ONT can be classed as trivial for the purpose of odour impact.

For larger releases it is necessary to assess their significance for odour nuisance. Because odour is readily detected over very short exposure times, typically a few seconds, it is necessary to estimate short term peak values of ground level concentrations, as shown in the bottom diagram in Figure 2.9. Hall and Kukadia, in *Approaches to the calculation of discharge stacks for odour control, (1994),* suggest that a factor of 10 is applied to account for very short term peak concentrations. This means multiplying by 10 the ground level concentrations predicted by any of the methods described above.

Because ONT concentrations for most highly odorous substances are well below concentrations likely to cause toxic effects, it is not necessary to apply a large safety margin when assessing the significance of the ground level concentration. Predicted concentrations in public areas below 0.1 x ONT may be regarded as trivial.

More information and other references on odour control is given in Appendices 2.3(d) and 2.3(e). Appendix 2.3(d) includes a table of typical odour emission figures for some industrial processes with the dilution factors required to reduce the emitted concentration to the OT concentration.

Releases to water

Dispersion of waterborne releases

For screening releases to water to assess significance, one of the following discharge situations should be selected as most closely representing the situation of your process:

(a) discharge to a river with mixing across the full width of the river;
(b) discharge to an estuary with mixing across the full width of the estuary at all states of the tide;
(c) discharge to a river with mixing limited to a plume from the discharge point;
(d) discharge to an estuary with mixing limited to a plume from the discharge point.

Estimates of dispersion in situations (a) and (b) are based on mass balance models. Estimates of dispersion in situations (c) and (d) are based on plume models.

Mass Balance Models

Figure 2.10 Mass balance modelling of dispersion in rivers and estuaries

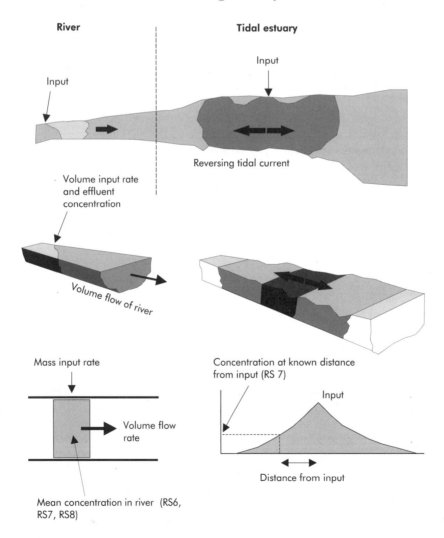

Note: RS 6, RS 7 and RS 8 are the References Sources we have used to derive the quick methods for estimating waterborne dispersion.

Figure 2.10 illustrates the basis for simple mass balance models of dilution in rivers and estuaries. The left hand diagrams apply to rivers and the right hand diagrams to estuaries. In both situations it is assumed that there has been sufficient time for the effluent to mix across the full width of the system. This is normally the case when the receiving water is shallow and fast moving with rapid mixing. If mixing across the width is incomplete, then a plume model, as described in the next section, should be used. The left hand upper illustration in Figure 2.10 shows a plan view of the spread of a continuous discharge from a location on one bank of a river. The middle illustration shows a three-dimensional view of the same situation, indicating that values of the effluent input rate and river volume flow rate are required for a simple model. The bottom illustration shows that the mean concentration in a steady flow depends on the mass of effluent entering a volume of river water as it passes the discharge point. In this simple model any further dilution of the discharged substance, by mixing along the length of the river, is ignored. Allowance should be made for any contribution to the overall concentration from upstream sources of the same substance.

An estuary discharge situation is shown on the right hand side of Figure 2.10. The top diagram shows a plan view of how the ebb and flood movement of the tide would spread a substance to either side of the discharge position. The middle three-dimensional diagrams show how the effluent is assumed to disperse uniformly across the width of the estuary, with concentrations decreasing upstream and downstream of the input point. With a continuous and constant rate of discharge, there is balance between the rate of input of the substance and the rates at which it is transported seawards by the river flow, and diffused both landwards and seawards by the oscillatory motion of the tides. The form of this longitudinal distribution in concentration, adopted in this simple model of the situation, is illustrated in the lower diagram.

Simple Plume Models

Figure 2.11 illustrates the situations in a river and an estuary when there is not complete mixing across the width of the water. In these cases a plume model must be used for estimating dilution.

Figure 2.11 Plume modelling of dispersion in rivers and estuaries

Instantaneous concentration distributions

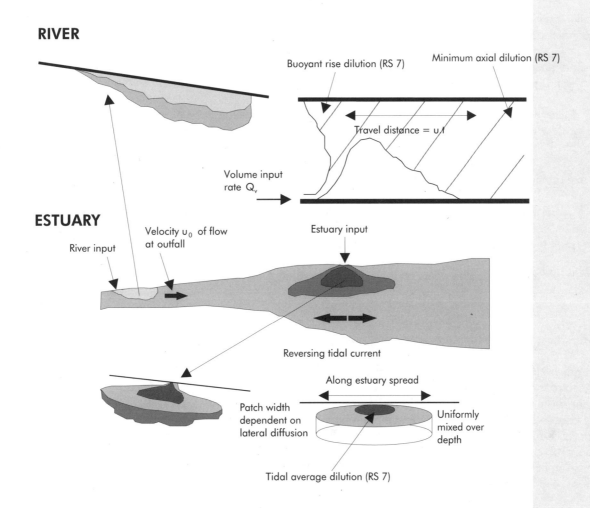

The middle illustration of Figure 2.11 is a plan view of effluent distributions resulting from inputs on one bank in the non-tidal and tidal estuary sections of a river.

The upper left hand diagram shows a plume widening in both the horizontal and vertical planes as the effluent is carried along by the river flow. In effluent plumes the highest concentrations generally occur along the axis of the plume and at the water surface. In contrast with the mass balance model, where complete lateral mixing is assumed, the existence of a plume means that lateral mixing is not complete. This means that concentrations of effluent in the river will vary across the river if measurements are taken relatively close to the discharge point. Another implication of plume formation is that the way an effluent is discharged can influence the rate of dilution. For example, if the effluent is relatively warm compared with the temperature of the river water, then a discharge at the river bed could obtain an appreciable degree of dilution as it rises to the surface. This is illustrated in the top right hand diagram. An estimate of the dilution attained during this buoyant rise stage may be needed, even in a first estimate of plume dilution. At greater distances from the discharge point the mode of input of the effluent has less effect on the dilution attained.

In an estuary, effluents are usually more buoyant than the saline waters and obtain a degree of dilution when rising to the surface from a discharge at the bed. The left-hand diagram of the lower pair in Figure 2.11 illustrates the three-dimensional concentration distribution resulting from the continuous input of an effluent into a tidal estuary. In a simple model this can be represented by an ellipsoidal form for lateral dispersion with uniform mixing over depth. This enables a first estimate of dilution to be made using a simple model in which the plume width is controlled solely by the tidal movement.

Simple methods for estimating water borne dispersion

(i) Reference source RS6 - *the Derivation of Quality Conditions for Effluents Discharged to Freshwaters,* by Price and Pearson, Anglian Water Authority, published by Water Pollution Control (1979)

This document provides a formula, based on mass balance, for discharges to freshwater rivers. It relates effluent flow and river flow to downstream concentrations of effluent in the river. It assumes complete mixing at the point of discharge and no deposition or degradation of the effluent in the river.

A fuller explanation of the formula and more information about the method and its limitations is given in Appendix 2.3 (f).

(ii) Reference source RS7 - *Discharge Consents and Compliance - The NRA's Approach to Control of Discharge to Water,* available from Environment Agency as Water Quality Series No.17 (1994).

This document provides a simple mass balance formula for estimating the concentration of an effluent in a river downstream of a discharge point. It also gives useful background information about the regulatory framework for water pollution control.

An explanation of the formula and more information about the document is provided in Appendix 2.3 (g).

(iii) Reference source RS8 - *Dispersion in Estuaries and Coastal Waters,* by R E Lewis, published by John Wiley (1997).

This book gives formulae for buoyant rise dilution and for dilution along the axis of an effluent plume.

Details of the formulae and notes on their use are given in Appendix 2.3 (h).

Releases to land

Deposition from airborne releases

The models described in Reference Sources RS1, RS2 and RS3 for estimating the ground level concentrations of substances released from chimneys all assume that there is no loss of material from the dispersing plume when it comes into contact with the ground. This simplifying assumption is a reasonable and conservative approach for estimating the concentrations that people would be exposed to. However, in practice material will be removed from the plume when it contacts the ground through impaction or absorption onto the ground and vegetation. If the emission from a chimney includes particulate matter containing harmful substances, e.g. dust containing heavy metals, an estimate should be made of the rate of deposition of the substance to check whether that would cause any harmful contamination of the soil or vegetation.

(i) Reference source RS 9 - **A Procedure to Include Deposition in the Model for Short and Medium Range Atmospheric Deposition of Radionuclides** published by NRPB (1981).

The "model" referred to in the title is the dispersion model from Reference Source RS 3. Like RS 3, this report is also applicable to non-radioactive gaseous and fine particulate matter. It provides a method for extending the use of the RS 3 model to estimate the rates of dry and wet deposition of fine particles onto the ground from a dispersing plume. It provides a relationship between the concentration of a substance in the plume at ground level and its rate of deposition. The main features of the report, with a look-up table, are given in Appendix 2.3(j).

Accumulation of deposited substances in soil

Environmental quality criteria for soil are expressed in terms of concentrations of substances in the surface layer of soil, usually as mg/kg (or ppm by weight). To convert from deposition rate in mg/m²/day to mg/kg the following formula may be used:

$$PC_{mg/kg} = \frac{f}{d \times \rho} \times T$$

Where:
- f = deposition flux of substance PC (mg/day/m²)
- d = mixing depth for substance (typically 0.075m)
- ρ = soil density (typically 1000 kg/m³)
- T = likely operational time of process (days)

This simple formula assumes no removal of the substance from the surface layer of soil by leaching or degradation. This is reasonable for persistent substances, such as heavy metals and very stable organic compounds but would over-estimate the build-up of substances that degrade more readily in soil. However, in the context of IPC/IPPC applications, it is very unlikely that airborne releases of degradable substances would lead to any significant contamination of soil if their concentrations in air were controlled to levels that satisfy the EQCs for those substances in air.

Deposition and accumulation in soil from direct spreading of wastes on land

Waste disposal by spreading onto agricultural land is only an option for waste materials that help to improve soil structure and fertility. It is most commonly used for disposing of sludge from sewage treatment works. Certain wastes from animal and vegetable processing operations in the food industry, wastes from paper pulp production and waste gypsum are also suitable for disposal in this way. The DoE Code of Practice for Agriculture Use of Sewage Sludge sets out the following general criteria for sludge disposal to agricultural land:

(a) there is no conflict with good agricultural practice;
(b) the long term viability of agricultural activities is maintained;
(c) public nuisance and water pollution are avoided;
(d) human, animal or plant health is not put at risk.

These criteria are also valid for other types of industrial wastes used in agriculture.

In comparison to emissions to air and discharges to water, dispersion of wastes in soil is extremely slow. Moreover there is no dilution between *source* and *target*, since the waste material is put directly onto or into the surface layer of soil. The general framework for environmental analysis (Figure 1.6) is still valid in principle for assessing the environmental impact of this method of waste disposal, but the approach has to be modified.

Where wastes are used in agriculture the rate of application must be controlled to maintain soil quality and fertility and to prevent unacceptable concentrations of substances that are potentially harmful in soil. Such substances are referred to a "potentially toxic elements (PTE) " in the DoE Code of Practice.

The EQCs for substances in soil information in Appendix 2.3(d) includes the maximum permissible concentrations of PTEs in soil after the application of sewage sludge from the DoE Code of Practice. Maximum permissible average annual rates of PTE addition, as kg/ha, are also given.

At the time of writing (October 1998) the Environment Agency is reviewing the whole subject of waste disposal by land spreading (Ref. 5). If your process has wastes that may be suitable for land spreading you should discuss this with the Environment Agency at a very early stage in your project development programme.

References

5. Environment Agency Research & Development Technical Report P193, from WRc Publications.

Further references

Appendix 2.3(k) gives a list of other useful references dealing with the control of releases to air and water and their dispersion in the environment.

Appendix 2.3(l) provide a list of models which may be used for more complex air and water dispersion modelling to assess the environmental effects of releases which are not screened out as *trivial,* using the simple methods described in this chapter.

2.4   Thresholds of triviality and significance

This section provides guidance for:

- selecting the appropriate environmental quality criteria (EQC) for a released substance;
- setting environmental quality thresholds (EQT) for categorising the significance of concentrations of released substances in the environment;
- comparing the results of simple dispersion estimates with the EQT to assess the significance of the release, i.e. whether it is trivial and no further analysis is required, or whether it is more significant, warranting more detailed assessment of its potential environmental impact.

Selecting Environmental Quality Criteria

The explanation of the term EQC in section 2.2 describes the various ways in which EQCs are derived and published. Section 2.2 also makes the point is made that careful consideration must be given to selecting the most appropriate EQC for each release situation. To recap in general terms, the following aspects must be considered:

- the EQC should be based on effects on the most sensitive receptor that is likely to be exposed in the release situation.
- the averaging time for which the EQC applies, e.g. annual mean, maximum allowable concentration, etc., should correspond to the release pattern, e.g. continuous, intermittent.
- the presence of any very sensitive receptors in the local environment, e.g. hospitals or SSSIs that would warrant applying an additional safety factor to an EQC.

Figure 2.12 sets out a procedure to help you select the most appropriate EQC for each release situation.

Figure 2.12 Selection of EQCs

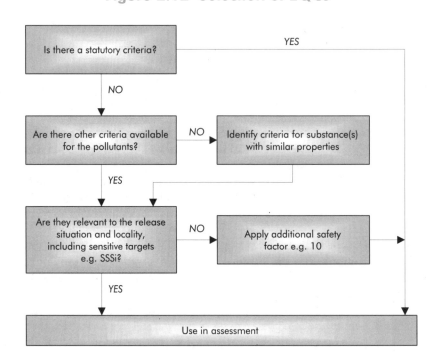

The outcome of the procedures for identifying release situations (section 2.2) and making simple dispersion calculations (section 2.3) will be estimates of the maximum concentration of each substance released to air or to water which is likely to impact on a sensitive receptor within range of the release. This concentration is the *Process Contribution (PC)*.

The reliability of the estimation of **PC** depends on:

- how well the release is characterised in terms of substance type, concentration, release profile (i.e. rate, frequency and duration of release, including variations and upsets), the total load released to the environment and any partitioning between receiving media;
- the dispersion modelling method used (e.g. rule of thumb, look-up table or chart, simple model, sophisticated model, etc. - see section 2.3);
- the quality of input data (e.g. locally measured meteorological data or data from similar site assumed; comprehensive or limited data on water flow rates; release rates measured or estimated, etc.);
- any approximations adopted (e.g. building effects not considered, no calculation of release profile carried out, etc.)

If a released substance is likely to be already present in the local environment from other sources, the procedures described in Chapter 3 should be used to make preliminary estimates of the existing or *ambient concentration (AC)*.

The sum of these (PC + AC) is the expected new concentration of the substance in the local environment - the *Predicted Environmental Concentration (PEC)*.

Another measure, which should be available from the **emission inventory**, is the *Release Concentration (RC)*. This is the concentration of a released substance in the emission to air or discharge to water at the release point - in the vent to atmosphere or in the discharge pipe to water.

Figure 2.13 is a summary of these measures and their relationship in the overall process of *Environmental Analysis* and *Assessment*. In effect, this table shows the possible outputs, for each **release situation**, of the procedures that have been described in this chapter.

Figure 2.13 The measures in environmental analysis and assessment

Environmental Analysis				Environmental Assessment
Background	Process Release	Dispersion Field	Environmental Load	Environmental Quality Criterion (EQC)
Ambient Concentration (AC) in absence of process	Release Concentration (RC)	Process Contribution (PC)	Predicted Environmental Concentration (PEC = AC + PC)	Statutory or guideline value most appropriate for the release situation and locality

From these measures the following ratios can be compiled:

$$\frac{RC}{EQC} \quad \frac{PC}{EQC} \quad \frac{PEC}{EQC} \quad \text{and} \quad \frac{PC}{AC}$$

The next paragraphs describe how these ratios can be used to assess the significance of each release situation.

In cases where the substance(s) released are not likely to be already present in the environment the PEC may be assumed to be the same as the PC.

Suggested Threshold Levels for Triviality and Significance

The basis for the recommendations in this section are:

- A release is *trivial* if it has no realistic potential to cause harm in the environment.
- A release is *significant*, to a greater or lesser extent, if it has some potential to cause harm to anything in the receiving environment.

The question of triviality and significance is not clear cut, except at the extremes of the range. A scale of significance is proposed, based on *threshold values* of the ratios of RC or PC or PEC to EQC. The diagram in Figure 2.14 shows the *threshold values* and corresponding levels of significance we recommend for assessing the significance of a release.

The terms used for the levels of significance - ***trivial, marginal, medium significance*** and *high* ***significance*** - are only intended as broad indicators for determining whether more detailed analysis is needed to assess the potential environmental effects of a release. The term ***marginal*** is used for releases that could be *trivial* in one situation but might be *medium significance* in another, depending on local circumstances.

Figure 2.14 Assessing the significance of releases

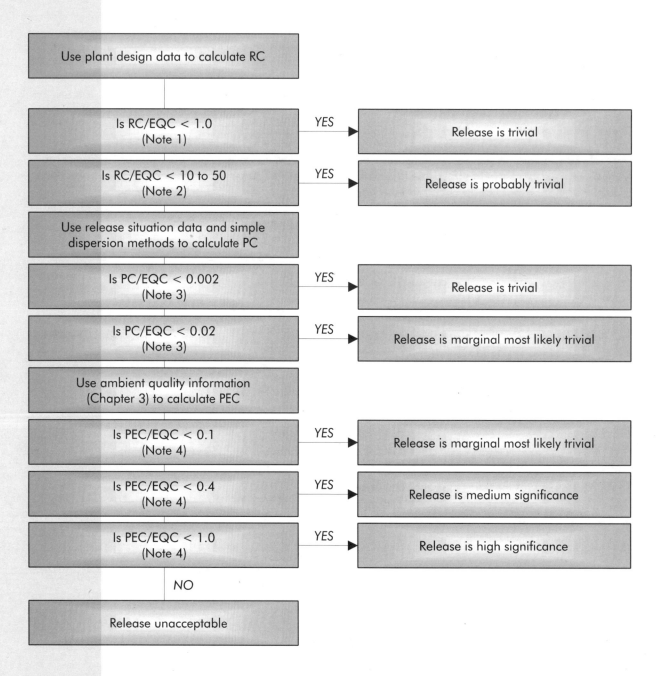

Notes on Figure 2.14

NOTE 1

If the RC < EQC, then the release cannot cause a PC greater than the EQC. For most releases to air or water, there will be rapid dilution in the environment to a small fraction of the EQC. The release is likely to be *trivial*. The operator must be sure that RC will remain at an acceptably low level.

NOTE 2

If the RC/EQC < n, where n is between 1 and about 10 to 50, the release can usually be classified as trivial since any well designed stack or water discharge point should routinely deliver 10 to 50 dilutions within a very restricted mixing zone. However this criterion only applies when it is certain that the release will be rapidly dispersed in the receiving environment. This may not be the case if:

- A stack release is subject to building downdraught or other air flow effects which cause early plume grounding;
- The stack release interacts with plumes containing the same pollutant from other stacks;
- The receiving environment already contains appreciable concentrations of the released pollutants;
- The flow rate of the receiving water is not at least 10 to 50 times greater than the discharge flow rate.

As a general rule, for a release to be judged as *trivial* on the basis of RC/EQC < n, n can be up to 50 for an airborne release from a vent clear of buildings and up to 10 for an effluent discharging to a watercourse. However, for airborne releases from vents with poor dispersion characteristics, e.g. where building effects occur, n should be no more than 10.

NOTE 3

If the PC/EQC is below the levels of 0.002 or 0.02, then the release should be classed as *trivial* or *marginal* respectively. At these levels the PC is a very small fraction of the EQC and, since EQCs (particularly statutory values) are always established with safety margins, is not likely to result in any adverse effects in the environment.

NOTE 4

The use of the ratio PEC/EQC indicates that the significance of the release is based on the resulting total environmental load (i.e. the contribution from the process plus any ambient concentration). The threshold values for the ratio PEC/EQC, to give the categories *marginal, medium significance* and *high significance*, are based on the recommendations of an EAC working group.

Although we recommend specific bands of the values of the ratios RC/EQC, PC/EQC and PEC/EQC to categorise the significance of a release, in practice the decision process is not so precise. If there are good reasons for adopting a more (or less) cautious approach in your local situation the significance categories should be adjusted to reflect those circumstances.

The ratio PC/AC may also be used as an indicator of significance for commonly occurring pollutants. If PC/AC < 0.02 the release may be treated as *trivial* in relation to existing levels of pollution.

Practical Implications

The purpose of the above procedure is to determine whether further analysis is necessary to assess the acceptability of a proposed release. More detailed and more reliable analysis is necessary as the potential to cause harm increases. The requirements fall into the following areas:

- further analysis and assessment using less conservative and more realistic models;
- more detailed estimation or measurement of process releases and ambient concentration data;
- an increasing need to demonstrate that the process can reliably meet the release limits likely to be set in the IPC authorisation through process specifications and/or controls and regular or continuous release monitoring and possibly environmental monitoring;
- an increasing probability of the need for reductions in amounts of substances released with improvement programmes and timetables specified in IPC authorisations.

The table in Figure 2.15 indicates the practical implications that are likely to follow for each category of significance.

Figure 2.15   Practical Implications following Assessment of Levels of Significance

Assessment				Practical Implications		
RC/ EQC	PC/ EQC	PEC/ EQC	Environmental Effect	Analysis and Assessment Required	Control Required	Improvement Programme Required
		> 1.0	Unacceptable, except in most unusual circumstances	Authorisation very unlikely. Accurate models and data. Ambient quality monitoring.	If authorised, high level of process plant and release control; continuous emission monitoring.	Major improvement on tight time-scales; new abatement system and/or fundamental process review
		0.4 - 1.0	High significance	Accurate models and data required. Probable need for ambient quality monitoring.	High level of process plant and release control; continuous monitoring of emissions.	Early improvement programme for substantial reduction of release
		0.1 - 0.4	Medium significance	Accurate models and data required. Possible need for ambient quality monitoring.	High level of process plant and release control, continuous monitoring of emissions.	Longer term improvement plans
	< 0.02	0.01 - 0.1	Marginal	Realistic models and data required.	High level of process plant and release control; regular emission monitoring.	Improvement programme unlikely
	< 0.002	< 0.01	Trivial	Approximate, conservative methods and data acceptable.	Good process control coupled with occasional monitoring.	None
Approx. 1 to 10 -50			Trivial	Approximate, conservative methods and data acceptable.	Process control monitoring and infrequent emission monitoring to check performance.	None
< 1.0			Trivial	Approximate, conservative methods and data acceptable.	Process control monitoring and infrequent emission monitoring to check performance.	None

Chapter 3 Determining ambient quality in the area affected by releases

3.1 Introduction

Section 1.4 in Chapter 1 explains why information on the *ambient quality* of the environment around an IPC process is needed for *environmental analysis* and *assessment*. This chapter describes a structured approach to help you decide what information you need, how to obtain it and how to use it in assessing the environmental effects of releases. The procedure we recommend will also help to give you a good understanding of the condition of the local environment that your process will affect and provide a sound basis for your IPC application and any discussions with the Environment Agency.

Section 3.2 examines the need for ambient quality information. It provides guidance to help you decide on the level of detail and certainty required in ambient quality data and describes how to use the data for calculating the *predicted environmental concentrations* of released substances for your IPC application.

Section 3.3 gives general guidance for determining ambient quality data and sections 3.4, 3.5 and 3.6 show you how to apply this general guidance to obtain appropriate ambient quality data for air, water and land respectively.

The worked example in Chapter 4 illustrates the application of this guidance.

3.2 The role of ambient quality data in environmental analysis for IPC

Figure 3.1, which is the framework diagram (Figure 1.5) from Chapter 1, shows that you need information on *ambient quality* at two stages in the overall procedure. Firstly, you may need limited information for the initial screening of releases, using the procedures described in Chapter 2. Then you will need more detailed and more reliable information for full assessment of the significant releases. At both stages you may need *ambient quality data* for each of the three environmental compartments (air, water and soil) that are likely to be contaminated by releases from your IPC process.

Figure 3.1 The role of ambient quality in an IPC application

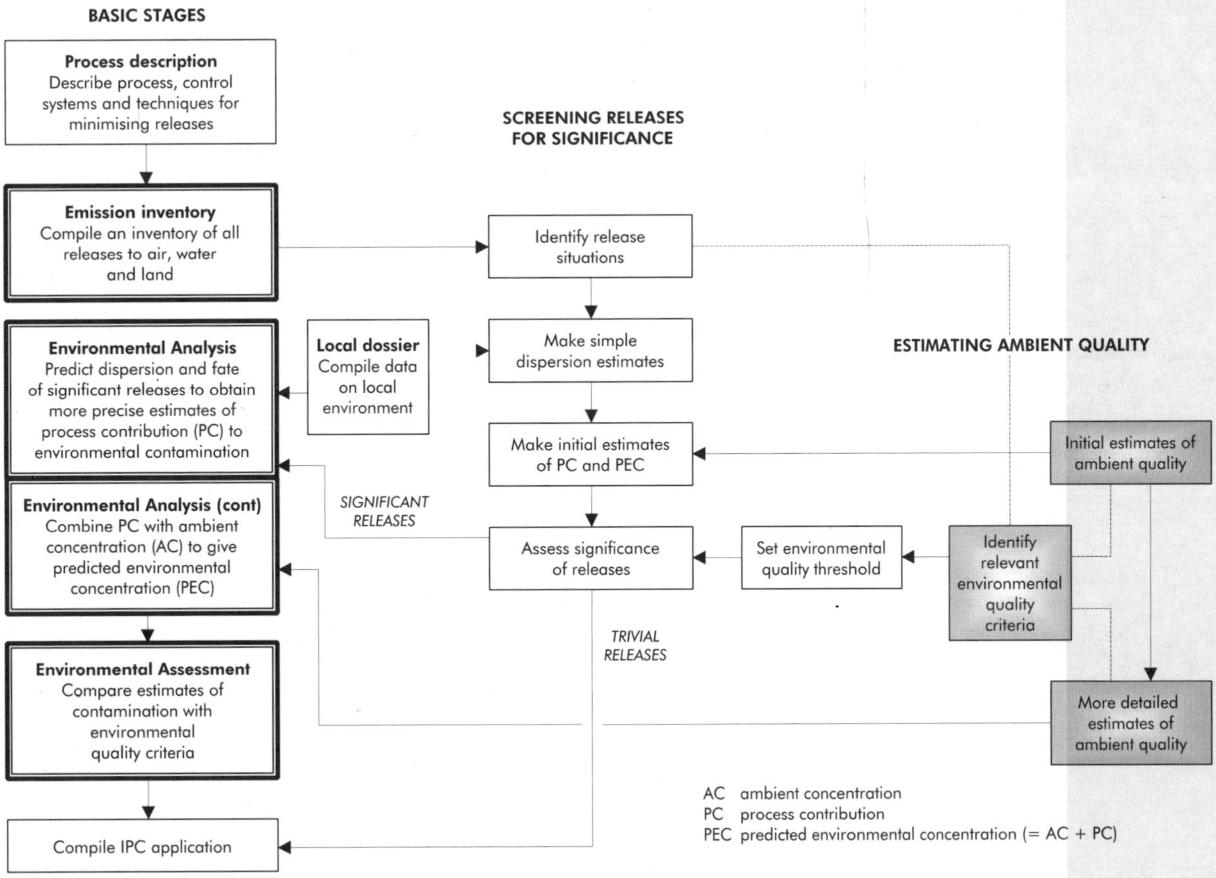

The first point to consider is the level of detail and certainty that you require for ambient data. This depends on how close the PC is to the EQC. In terms of the scale of significance used in Chapter 2 (section 2.4), the more significant the release the more important it is to have reliable information about ambient quality. This is illustrated in Figure 3.2.

Figure 3.2 Relationship between PC, AC, PEC and EQC

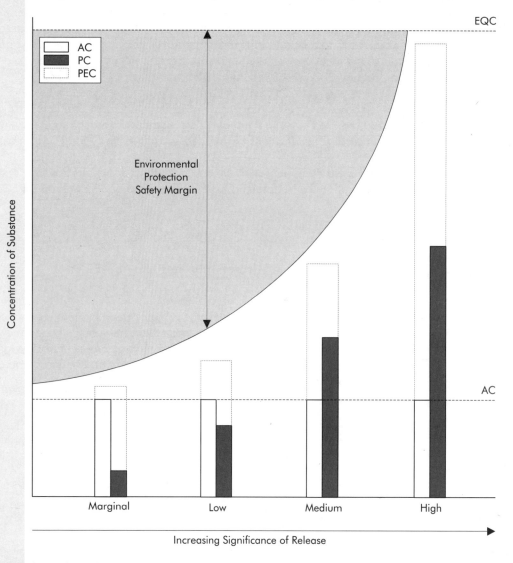

The diagram shows how the margin of safety for environmental protection is lower for the more significant releases. This means that there is less room for uncertainty about the AC if you are seeking IPC authorisation for a process with medium or high significance releases. The same *environmental threshold criteria* (from Figure 2.4) that you used for assessing the significance of releases can be used as a guide to the level of detail and certainty required for ambient data. Figure 3.3 shows a table relating significance of a release to ambient data requirements.

Figure 3.3 Significance of release and ambient data requirements

Threshold of significance	Significance level	Ambient data requirements
PEC/EQC < 0.1	Marginal	Approximate estimates usually adequate
PEC/EQC < 0.4	Medium significance	Reliable data from similar locations
PEC/EQC < 1.0	High significance	High degree of certainty and specific to location. Current monitoring results in sensitive situations

The next section provides some general principles and guidance for determining ambient quality at the levels of detail and certainty described in the right hand column of the table in Figure 3.3.

3.3 How to determine and apply ambient quality

Sources of ambient quality data

The aim of this advice is to help you obtain the most appropriate data in the most cost-effective way, at the level of certainty required for each significant release and over the area covered by the *process footprint.*

In order of increasing detail and reliability, possible sources of ambient quality data are:

- Typical UK values for certain location types, e.g. urban, rural. These are mainly applicable to air and soil.
- River water classifications.
- Extrapolating or interpolating from measured values in nearby or similar locations. This approach is mainly applicable to air.
- Recent measurements of ambient concentrations in the area affected by the releases.
- New measurement programmes specifically designed to provide ambient quality data for the proposed project. This is exceptional and only likely for large-scale developments in sensitive areas.

Sections 3.4, 3.5 and 3.6 describe how these sources of information can be used to determine ambient quality data for air, water and soil respectively.

Units and averaging times

Ambient quality is usually characterised in units of concentration (amount of substance per unit volume, e.g. parts per billion by volume - ppbv, mg/m^3, mg/l etc), or in a weight for weight format (e.g. mg/kg). For air and water this will be associated with a defined timescale or averaging period, i.e. the period over which a sample is taken.

Another important aspect in reporting and using the results of either ambient quality monitoring or dispersion modelling is the *resolution* of the measurements or estimates. This term refers to the level of detail measured or estimated. There are two elements to the *resolution*:

- The averaging period over which the concentration is measured or estimated. This can vary from short periods, such as 15 minute or hourly means, to much longer periods, such as daily, fortnightly, or annual means.
    - Measurements taken over short time periods provide a large number of data points and a very detailed picture of the variation of concentration with time. This is *high resolution* data.
    - Measurements taken over long time periods provide a less detailed picture of the variation of concentration with time. This is *low resolution* data.

- The percentile value that is quoted.

    This is the percentage of measured or estimated values that fall within a specified limit. When an EQC is expressed in this way it specifies a limit but allows a stated percentage of individual measurements to exceed that limit. For example, in the current EU Directive for nitrogen dioxide in air, the 98th percentile of 1-hour means must not exceed 200 mg/m^3. This means that 98% of hourly mean measurements must be at or below 200 mg/m^3 but 2% of measurements may exceed this level without breaching the limit.

Statutory EQCs for air quality for public health protection are usually expressed as a high percentile value of short term measurements <u>and</u> an annual mean value to provide protection against both acute and chronic effects (see Appendix 2.3(a)). Ambient quality monitoring results are published on the same basis for comparison. EQCs and ambient quality data for water are usually expressed as annual averages or 95th percentiles or maximum values. EQCs and ambient concentrations in soil do not involve any averaging period or timescales.

When you combine the predicted maximum concentration of a released substance (the PC) with the ambient quality (AC) and compare the result with an EQC to assess the acceptability of a release, all three measures must be in the same units, measured or estimated over the same averaging times and quoted at the same precision, i.e. they must all be at the same *resolution*. If all the data are not available at the same *resolution*, use the guidance in the following paragraphs to make appropriate adjustments.

Figure 3.4 illustrates averaging periods and percentiles to show how important it is to know the resolution of a reported value for ambient quality before using it in an environmental assessment.

Figure 3.4 Averaging times and percentiles

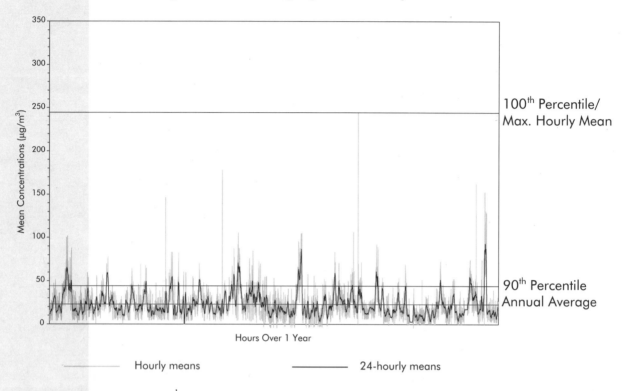

If ambient data is not available at the resolution used in the EQC, you may use it to make a conservative comparison, i.e. erring on the safe side, by applying the following approach:

- A shorter averaging period (higher resolution) is a more stringent alternative for a longer averaging period (lower resolution). For example, peak hourly measurements are always higher than peak 24 hour measurements.
- Higher percentiles are conservative alternatives for lower percentiles.

EQCs are expressed in terms of the resolution that is most appropriate for protecting sensitive species from harmful effects of the substance.

- Where a substance has immediate adverse effects (usually referred to as acute effects), then short term exposures above the harmful level must be avoided. In this case the EQC will be expressed as a short-term maximum value, e.g. 99.9th percentile of 15 minute mean values, or as a maximum allowable concentration which should never be exceeded.
- If the adverse effect is less immediate (usually referred to as chronic effects) the relevant measure of exposure is the average concentration over longer periods and minor short-term excursions can be tolerated. In these cases the EQC limit may be set as a longer term mean value with a less stringent percentile value, indicating that some exceedance can be tolerated for some of the time), such as 98th or 95th percentile of daily values.
- If a substance causes harm by exposure to very low levels over long periods, which is thought to be the case for some cancer causing substances, the EQC may be expressed as a long term average limit, such as an annual average value.
- Some substances cause more than one type of harmful effect in the environment, (e.g., at high enough concentrations, sulphur dioxide is a respiratory irritant, contributes to acidic deposition and causes damage to vegetation). In such cases the EQC may be expressed as a combination of limits at different resolutions to cater for the different effects or separate EQCs for the substance may be set for each purpose. The most appropriate one to use will usually be apparent from the information you have compiled to describe the *release situation* (see section 2.2).

(For a few categories of substances that contribute to global environmental effects, the EQC approach to environmental protection is not appropriate. This is the case for the so-called greenhouse gases, such as carbon dioxide and methane, and for persistent chlorinated compounds that deplete the stratospheric ozone layer. The environmental effects are related to total global emissions, rather than to local concentrations. Control is, or will be, exercised by national mass emission limits set by international agreements, such as the Montreal Protocol for reducing emissions of CFCs to stop damage to the stratospheric ozone layer, or the Kyoto agreement in 1997 which will lead to national programmes for reducing greenhouse gas emissions.)

When you combine ambient concentrations (AC) with PC to determine PECs, you should keep the following points in mind:

- Long-term, annual averages are additive, i.e. an annual average AC can be combined with an annual average PC as a representative estimate of annual average PEC.
- Short term averages and high percentiles are not necessarily additive because the conditions that produce the 98th percentile PC and the 98th percentile AC are likely to be different. Therefore adding these two values would be an extreme worst case and over estimate the most likely value of the PEC expressed as a 98th percentile value. This is particularly relevant for releases to air. Suggestions for dealing with this problem are given in Section 3.4.

Treatment of uncertainty

The Introduction to this book points out that environmental analysis and assessment is not an exact science. Measurements of concentrations of substances in the environment are never exact because of the imprecision of sampling techniques and analytical methods and the variable nature of the environmental media of air, water and soil. When you use estimates of ambient quality data in environmental assessment you should be aware of how reliable those estimates are. The diagram in Figure 3.2 and the table in Figure 3.3 show that the level of uncertainty that can be tolerated decreases as the PEC becomes closer to the EQC. The following paragraphs explain some of the main sources of uncertainty in ambient data and their implications for environmental assessment.

Uncertainty in environmental quality data

All sampling and analytical techniques and measuring instruments have inherent inaccuracies. As a general rule, the more measurements that are made for determining an average value over a period of time, the more reliable that value will be. For example, a continuous analyser sampling over a period of several years would provide the most reliable values of the typical hourly, daily, weekly or annual averages for that location. It would also provide the most reliable value of the absolute maximum concentration.

One of the practical problems in identifying relevant ambient quality data is the difficulty of finding reliable data at the required averaging time. Measuring short-term data for substances in air, such as hourly averages, requires sophisticated and expensive continuous monitoring equipment. Consequently such information is available for relatively few sites. Longer-term averages are more readily available. Sampling methods for measuring daily, fortnightly or monthly averages are in widespread use for monitoring common pollutants in air and water and the results can be used to compile annual averages.

The uncertainty associated with an annual average value is much less than that for a maximum short-term value, since the purpose of the latter is to detect short-term fluctuations as conditions vary. Figure 3.4 shows how a few high value short-term peaks have little effect on the annual average value, which is therefore subject to less uncertainty. All other things being equal, the annual average value at a monitoring station would not change significantly from one year to the next but the hourly peak value in one year might be several times higher, or lower, than in the previous year.

For much the same reasons, percentile values are more reliable when calculated from a larger data set. For a given data set, higher percentile values, such as the 99th percentile, are less reliable than lower percentiles.

When environmental assessment requires comparison of PEC with an EQC expressed in terms of a maximum short-term average value, such as a maximum or a high percentile of hourly mean values, there will be considerable uncertainty in the comparison if ambient concentrations (AC) at the same resolution have to be derived from small data sets or data at lower resolution. This should be highlighted in the assessment because the AC values so derived are likely to underestimate actual short-term peak concentrations.

Uncertainty in using environmental quality data

Ambient quality data of the right kind at the required resolution is seldom available at the location of a new process seeking IPC authorisation. You will have to make estimates, using whatever data is available.

For air, maps of ambient quality are available for specific pollutants (Ref. 9). These maps are compiled by interpolating between sites where measurements have been made and making allowances for the likely effects of known major sources. Such maps are helpful but must be used with caution.

All extrapolations of ambient quality data from one location to another, however similar they are, clearly add to the uncertainty of the estimate of AC. Reliability will also be lower if there is little or no knowledge of other pollutant sources in the local area.

Additional uncertainty arises when available ambient data are not at the required resolution and estimates have to be made using conversion factors from one averaging period to another. This is illustrated in section 3.4.

All these factors point to the need to err on the safe side when you are compiling values of AC for environmental assessment. As a general rule, use values at the higher end of the available measurements. This will ensure that you are basing your assessment on worst case situations and provide assurance that you are not under estimating the risks of harmful environmental impacts from your new process.

What to do if Ambient Quality approaches EQC

There may be situations where the ambient concentration is close to or even exceeds the EQC without any addition from the new process. This is most likely to occur for common air pollutants in areas with heavy industrial activity and high traffic volumes, or for waterborne discharges to heavily polluted watercourses.

In this situation your initial comparison of EQC with PC + AC = PEC may indicate that a particular release would not be acceptable in an IPC application. However other considerations may still allow your development to go ahead, for example:

- If the process contribution is very small, say <0.2% of the EQC, the release may be regarded as trivial and therefore acceptable.
- Is the location or time of peak concentrations from the process likely to coincide with the location or time of the highest ambient concentrations? If not, the new process may be acceptable.
- Are there planned developments and changes in the locality that will lead to lower ambient concentrations in the near future, e.g., another significant source of the same pollutant is to cease before the proposed new process starts up.

You should discuss all these considerations, and any other site specific issues affecting local pollution levels, with the Environment Agency inspector at an early stage in your project development programme to ensure that,if you proceed, your IPC application is likely to be authorised.

When to consider direct measurement of ambient quality

For a limited number of major projects in sensitive locations it may not be sufficient to estimate the local ambient quality from available data. For example, if you are considering a new fuel burning installation in an area with high traffic density where there is already concern that the air quality limit for nitrogen dioxide might not be met. Another example might be a new process with an effluent for discharge to an estuary where there is concern about the effect on fish stocks and very little reliable data is available on the current water quality in the estuary.

In such cases you should consider carrying out local environmental monitoring to reduce uncertainties and to provide reliable ambient quality data to support your IPC application.

Direct measurement of ambient quality is a specialist task, expensive and time consuming. Before you make any detailed plans, discuss the project with the Environment Agency to agree the specific data requirements and how these might be met most economically. The design of any monitoring programme has to be specifically tailored for the location. A comprehensive plan should be clearly established at the outset. It may be appropriate to make use of existing data supplemented by additional selective measurement. If there are local interests with concerns about the development you should involve them in the monitoring plans.

A major factor in determining what measurements you should make is, again, how close the estimated PC is to the relevant EQC. The closer the predicted concentration of the pollutant is to the EQC, the more important the accuracy and reliability in estimating the ambient concentration becomes (see Figures 3.2 and 3.3).

Sections 3.4, 3.5 and 3.6, with their appendices, contain further details and sources of information on setting up measurement programmes for air, water and soil respectively. General points that apply to any environmental measurement programme are:

- Clearly establish information needs and objectives.
- Determine specific data requirements based on the relevant EQC(s). This will define averaging periods and precision required for measurements.
- Plans for a sampling and analysis programme should cover certain key aspects:

  - The pattern of sampling sites. This should be based on the expected process footprint of the released substances with maximum coverage where maximum concentrations of released substances are expected.
  - Expected variations in ambient levels and the *resolution* needed for comparison with the EQCs of the relevant substances. At least 1 year of data is required to provide a reliable annual average value. Short-term measurements, such as hourly mean values, ideally require several years of measurements for reliable values in order to take account of seasonal variations. However this is unlikely to be practicable for a new development and shorter monitoring periods during the seasons most likely to give highest values may be acceptable.
  - Sampling and analysis techniques. The accuracy and detail required in terms of averaging periods, detection levels, type of pollutant etc. will determine which techniques should be selected.
  - Statistical techniques and data analysis - reporting arrangements.
  - Quality control arrangements - validation - Good Laboratory Practice.
  - Whether a feasibility study or pilot sampling study should form part of the programme design.

- It may be possible to set up a programme with other parties (such as other industries and local authorities) to share costs and, if necessary, increase coverage (both geographically and for the number of pollutants).
- The start-up of any new processes with similar releases in the surrounding area during the monitoring period should be noted and the impact assessed.

3.4 Ambient air quality

General considerations

Ambient air quality is the existing concentrations of substances in air measured at ground level, i.e. where people, plants and animals are exposed.

Measured values of short-term concentrations in air can vary by orders of magnitude over a period of minutes. You must know the averaging period of any quoted value before using it for comparison with an EQC. The main aim of the guidance which follows is to show you how to make best use of available information on ambient air quality to estimate the AC for the process location at the same *resolution* as the relevant EQC.

If the EQC is expressed as an annual average value you should have estimated the PC as an annual average value. If ambient air quality data for the substance is available as an annual average value at the location, you can then calculate the predicted environmental concentration (PEC), as an annual average value, by simply adding the annual average values of PC and AC.

If the EQC is expressed as a short-term value, e.g. an hourly or daily mean value, the values of PC and AC must also be at the same resolution. However, you should not add a maximum short-term PC value to a maximum short-term AC value to derive the maximum short-term PEC; the reason being that the atmospheric conditions causing the maximum value of PC at a given location are often different from the conditions causing the maximum value of AC at the same location.   This is particularly so for a PC from a stack emission and an AC that is mainly attributable to ground level emissions from vehicles.

An important feature of ambient air quality data is that it is possible to make reasonable estimates of the concentrations of common air pollutants at a one location by extrapolating from available measurements at other locations. You can do this when monitoring sites are near your new process site or are sufficiently similar in terms of the intensity of urban development and industrial activities. The next paragraphs give guidance for doing this.

In many urban areas the ambient concentrations of common air pollutants, such as nitrogen dioxide (NO_2) and suspended particulates (PM_{10}) currently exceed the EQC levels we quote. This does not mean that no new industrial development will be permitted in these areas and you should still follow the environmental assessment method we recommend in this chapter. However you should discuss the implications of the situation with the Environment Agency and the local authority at an early stage. There may be a local air quality improvement programme that you would have to take into account in assessing the likely acceptability of the airborne releases from your process.

A structured approach for assessing ambient air quality

Figure 3.5 shows a series of steps that you can follow to make the most appropriate estimate of ambient air quality as cost-effectively as possible.

Figure 3.5 Steps for the assessment of ambient air quality

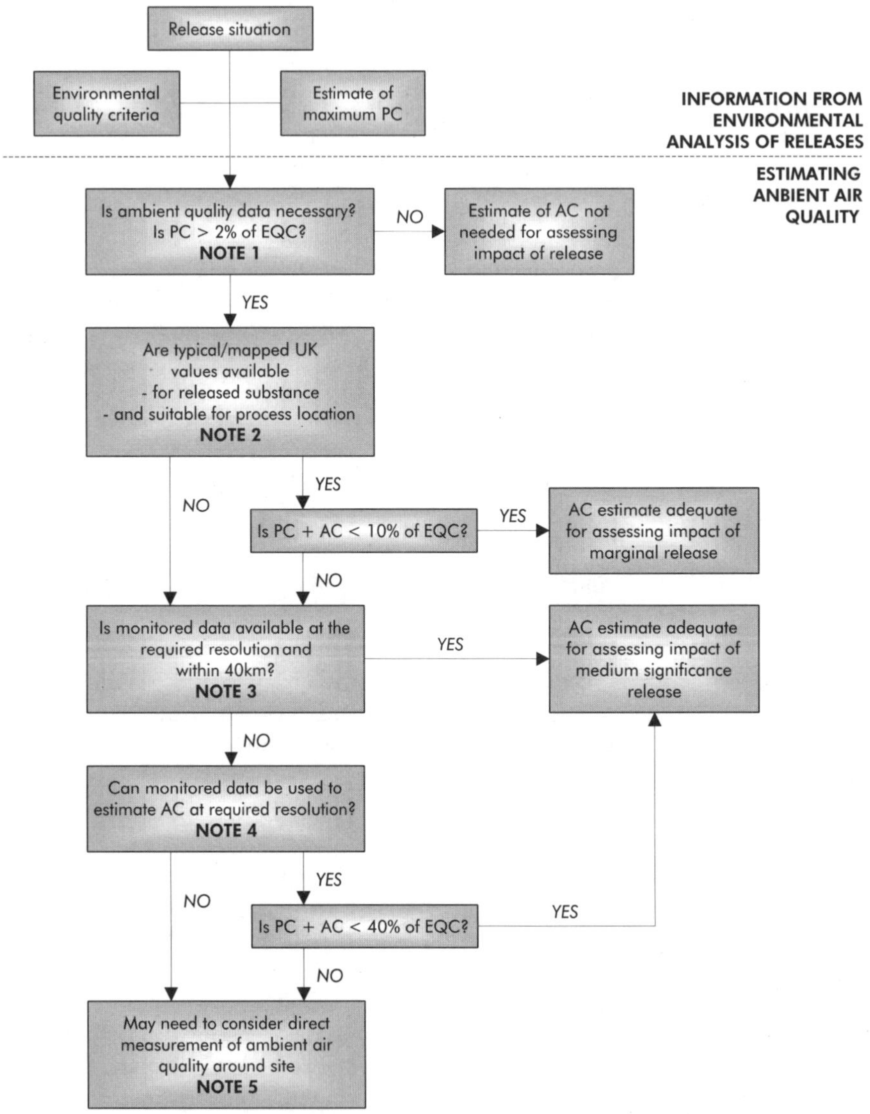

The following notes explain how to the use the procedure in Figure 3.6.

NOTE 1

There will be cases in which a reliable estimate of ambient air quality is not necessary. If the PC is less than 2% of the EQC the release will have been classed as *trivial* because its effect on local air quality is probably not detectable. Ambient quality is also not relevant if the released substance is unique to your process and unlikely to be present in the air from any other sources. However, for most releases of common air pollutants that you have assessed to be *significant,* you will need to make an estimate of the ambient concentration.

NOTE 2

Figure 3.3, relating significance of release to ambient data requirements, indicates that if the PC is less than 10% of the EQC the ambient data estimate can probably be based on typical UK values to give an order of magnitude estimate. If the resulting PEC is still less than 10% of the EQC this estimate of AC is adequate.

Figure 3.6 provides typical UK ambient concentrations for the common air pollutants measured in the DETR's national air quality monitoring networks. For each pollutant values of annual mean and 98th percentile and 90th percentile of hourly means are shown. The values are shown for 6 types of monitoring sites:

Kerbside   Within 5 m of a major road

Major city centre   A large urban centre with many intersecting busy roads

Major suburban area   A mainly residential area more than 50 m from a major road

Small town   A town centre, mainly residential with some A-class roads

Partially developed   Small towns and villages, widely dispersed

Rural   Open country. No sources within 1km of the site

Select the category of location which best describes the area around your process; then use the values from Figure 3.6 for the AC of the air pollutants that feature in your significant releases. In some cases the selection of monitoring site category may not be clear cut. A conservative approach is to use the more polluted category for your assessment; alternatively a value of AC may be estimated by bracketing your process site between the two nearest categories.

Figure 3.6 Typical ambient concentrations for air pollutants in the UK

Typical Annual Mean Background Concentrations

	SO_2 ppb	NO_x ppb	NO_2 ppb	O_3 ppb	lead µg m⁻³	PM10 µg m⁻³	CO ppb	benzene ppb	1, 3 butadiene ppb
Kerbside	10	150	35	-	0.16	30	1.8	2	0.5
Major city centre	8	65	28	15	0.08	26	0.6	1.5	0.3
Major suburban centre	7	50	24	17	0.05	24	0.5	1.2	0.2
Small town	6	40	18	19	0.04	22	0.45	0.8	0.2
Partially developed	3	25	10	25	0.025	20	0.2	0.4	0.2
Rural	2	8	5	30	0.005	10	0.1	0.2	0.1

	SO$_2$ ppb	NO$_x$ ppb	NO$_2$ ppb	O$_3$ ppb	lead μg m^{-3}	PM10 μg m^{-3}	CO ppb	benzene ppb	1, 3 butadiene ppb
Kerbside	40	350	80	-	-	85	4.0	6.5	1.4
Major city centre	35	240	60	40	-	75	2.0	5.5	1.2
Major suburban centre	30	200	55	50	-	70	1.8	4.5	1.0
Small town	25	175	50	56	-	60	1.6	4.0	1.0
Partially developed	15	100	35	58	-	45	0.6	1.5	0.5
Rural	8	30	20	60	-	35	0.4	1.0	0.5

Values are 98th percentile of hourly means.

Typical 90th percentile Concentrations

	SO$_2$ ppb	NO$_x$ ppb	NO$_2$ ppb	O$_3$ ppb	lead μg m^{-3}	PM10 μg m^{-3}	CO ppb	benzene ppb	1, 3 butadiene ppb
Kerbside	20	300	65	-	-	60	3.2	4.0	0.8
Major city centre	16	130	50	30	-	50	1.2	2.6	0.6
Major suburban centre	15	100	40	32	-	44	0.9	2.2	0.4
Small town	13	80	35	24	-	40	0.8	1.6	0.3
Partially developed	7	40	25	28	-	34	0.5	0.8	0.2
Rural	4	15	12	42	-	16	0.3	0.6	0.1

Values are 90th percentile of hourly means unless otherwise stated.

[1] Data for 1-2 years at 3-6 sites per category are used to calculate the "typical value" estimates. The data for SO$_2$, NO$_2$, NO$_x$, O$_3$, PM10, benzene, CO and 1,3 butadiene were derived from hourly mean data from automatic instruments which form part of the UK Automatic Networks. Lead is derived from both weekly, monthly and quarterly means at various sites measured by a filter sampler.

Background Concentration Maps

Maps of annual mean ambient concentrations are now available for PM$_{10}$, NO$_2$, CO, Benzene and SO$_2$. These maps have been produced for the UK on a 1 km by 1 km grid for 1996, and are available on the Internet at:

http://www.environment.detr.gov.uk/airq/aqinfo.htm

The maps are based on interpolation of rural measurements and simple modelling of dispersed low-level point sources, using national emission inventories. You can zoom in on the map to look more closely at any region that interests you, and by clicking on the map you can obtain figures for concentrations around any point. This provides an estimate of the average annual concentration over the general area of your process site but is too broadbrush to take account of very local sources. If your point of maximum PC is likely to be close to a major road or overlap with other local industrial sources, you should make due allowance.

Using typical and mapped values

1. For substances with long-term EQCs, e.g. annual average limits

   (a) Use the typical values of annual average concentrations (from Figure 3.6 or the air quality maps) to estimate the AC annual average value for your process site.

   (b) Add this to the PC, which has been calculated as an annual average, to give the PEC as an annual average figure. Make sure that all the figures are in the same units. As Figure 3.6 shows, some substances are reported in ppb, others in mg/m³. Figure 3.7 shows how to convert from one to the other.

   (c) If PC + AC = PEC <10% of EQC, the annual average value of AC you have used is generally sufficiently precise for an IPC application, since the variation around the typical value is unlikely to be more than a factor of 2 or 3. However the Environment Agency may ask for a more detailed assessment of AC, even if PEC < 10% of EQC, in situations where general pollution levels are already high or where several industrial processes are contributing to levels of the particular substance.

   (d) If PC + AC = PEC > 10% of EQC, proceed to the next step in Figure 3.5

Figure 3.7 Converting ambient quality units

Conversion of ppb to µg/m³ can be undertaken using the following equation, assuming an air temperature of 15°C:

$$C\left(\frac{\mu g}{m^3}\right) = \frac{C(ppb)}{1000}\left(\frac{m_m}{0.0224}\right) \times \left(\frac{273}{288}\right)$$

where: C   = concentration
          m_m = molar mass (see table below for examples)

An alternative air temperature may be used by altering the value (288) in the above equation to another temperature in degrees kelvin (°K = °C + 273).

Molecular mass of selected pollutants

Pollutant	m_m (g/mole)
Benzene	78
1, 3 Butadiene	54
Carbon monoxide	28
Nitrogen dioxide	46
Lead	207
Sulphur dioxide	64

2. For substances with short-term EQCs, e.g. 98th percentile of hourly means

   (a) We have already explained that simple addition of peak short-term values of AC and PC would usually over-estimate PEC, particularly when the released substances are emitted from a tall chimney. However, if the releases are at low level, such as a vent at roof level below 10m, it is more likely that peak values of PC and AC would coincide. In that situation it would not be unduly pessimistic to add 98th percentile of hourly (or daily) mean values of PC to the corresponding 98th percentile values of AC to estimate the 98th percentile value of PEC.

(b) For the more typical industrial situation, where significant releases to air are from tall chimneys, either of the following approaches are recommended for estimating short-term PEC values:

90th percentile AC + 98th percentile PC = 98th percentile PEC
(AC being measured and PC being estimated at same averaging period as EQC)

or

2 x annual average AC + 98th percentile PC = 98th percentile PEC

These recommendations are more likely to over-estimate rather than under-estimate the PEC, i.e. they err on the safe side for estimating the significance of releases. Appendix 3.4(a) shows a computer simulation of AC, PC and PEC hourly values over one year to illustrate these alternative ways of estimating a PEC value for comparison with an EQC expressed as a percentile of short term measurements.

(c) If PC + AC = PEC <10% of EQC, this approach should be sufficiently precise for an IPC application.

(d) If PC + AC = PEC > 10% of EQC, proceed to the next step in Figure 3.6

NOTE 3

If typical UK values or maps are not available for the substance released, or if PC + AC = PEC > 10% of EQC when AC has been estimated using typical values, the next step is to see if there are any individual monitoring sites which could provide a more reliable basis for estimating AC in the vicinity of the new process.

Air quality may have been measured in the vicinity, either at sites within the National Monitoring Networks or as local monitoring surveys set up by local authorities or as local industry programmes. You can use these data, provided they are at the required resolution and reliable, to determine ambient concentration by following the methods for calculating PECs described in Note 2.

Data from the national networks consist of:

Automatic monitoring (continuous measurements)

* Hourly NO, NO_2, CO, PM_{10}, O_3 and 15 minute mean SO2

Non-automatic monitoring (lower resolution measurements)

* Daily smoke and sulphur dioxide data
* Monthly NO_2 diffusion tube data
* Annual Pb in air data
* The air pollution "A to Z", providing examples of measurements of ambient concentrations of 322 air pollutants.

Data from the national networks are available:

* On-line via the World Wide Web at:
  http://www.environment.detr.gov.uk/airq/airqinfo.htm
* On CD-ROM direct from Air and Environment Quality Division of the DETR.
* Published in Air Pollution in the UK, which contains summary data from the automatic network (Ref. 7).
* Published in Digest of Environmental Statistics, containing a wider range summary statistics (Ref. 8).
* Published in Air Quality A-Z, which summarises a wide range of pollutant concentrations, their origins, methods of measurement and site locations (Ref. 9).

When you are deciding whether a particular monitoring site would provide ambient quality data that would be representative of your process site you should consider the following points:

* If the monitoring site is located within the process footprint it is clearly suitable, but remember that it will be detecting releases from any existing operations on your site.

- If such a monitoring site is not available, which is generally the case, monitoring results from sites within a 40 km radius may be suitable.
- If the substance is not a common pollutant there may be very few monitoring sites with relevant data. This is the case for most metals and specific organic compounds. It is, nevertheless, worth looking at these monitoring sites to see if any are located in similar situations to your process site. If a representative monitoring site is identified, the data may be used.
- As was the case when using the "typical UK values" in Note 2, the environment of both the monitoring site and the process footprint area should be taken into account. For example, if the process footprint area is a rural area then a nearby rural monitoring site should be used. If there is no nearby monitoring site with similar characteristics, data from a site in a more polluted environment (e.g. urban rather than rural) could be used to give a conservative estimate of AC. The references of sources of data from the national monitoring networks also give information about the environment of the monitoring sites.
- Where the process footprint includes a variety of environments, it is worth looking at monitoring sites which are representative of the different environments within your process footprint to see what variation there is likely to be in ambient concentrations of the released substance you are assessing.
- If there are other major sources of the same substance in the area around your process site you should not base your estimate of AC on monitoring results from other locations. You will need up-to-date local data.
- Short-term air quality measurements, such as hourly values, are highly variable because of the frequent changes in wind speed and direction near ground level. More than one year's data are required for a reliable assessment of the pollution climate. If less than three years data are available, it is advisable to add 20% to the annual mean value as a safety factor.

Figure 3.8 Surrogate values for comparing low resolution measurements with higher resolution EQCs

Pollutant	Actual EQC	Surrogate EQC	Other Surrogate Factor to Achieve Actual EQC Resolution
SO_2	100ppb 99.9th Percentile of 15 minute means (NAQS Objective)	48ppb Daily maximum	-
NO_2	200μg/m³ 98th Percentile of hourly means (EU Limit Value)	-	Multiply annual average ambient data from automatic monitoring sites by factor of 2.5. This will give a representative 98th Percentile of hourly means
NO_2	21ppb Annual mean (NASQ Objective)	-	Monthly diffusion tube data can be used to provide an ambient annual mean
PM_{10}	50μg/m³ 99th Percentile of running 24hr means (NASQ Objective)	46μg/m³ 99th Percentile of daily means	-
CO	10ppm Maximum running 8-hour mean (NASQ Objective)	-	Divide maximum running 8-hour mean for NO_x (ppb) from urban centre/background sites by 100. This will give a representative CO concentration in ppm
Benzene	3ppb Maximum running annual mean (NASQ Objective)	4.5ppb Fixed annual mean	-

If there are no suitable monitoring sites that provide data at the required resolution you can make estimates of hourly or 15 minute means from lower resolution data, such as daily or monthly means. For example if a non-automatic monitoring site is more representative of your process site than the nearest automatic site, it may be better to estimate the short term ambient concentration for your process site using the lower resolution data from non-automatic monitoring site. The table in Figure 3.8 gives some relationships between lower resolution data and higher resolution standards that have been derived from automatic monitoring data (Ref 5). The "surrogate EQCs" are approximations to the EQC, but expressed at lower resolution. They can be used if AC data are only available at that lower resolution. The right hand column in Figure 3.8 gives other "surrogate factors" which you can be use in similar fashion.

If none of the methods described in Notes 1 - 4 provide a reasonable basis for estimating AC for your process, you should discuss the case with the Environment Agency.

In these circumstances you may have to arrange actual measurement of ambient quality to provide reliable values of AC in support of your IPC application. (This activity is separate from any requirement the Environment Agency may make for monitoring the environmental impact of a new or existing process as part of the condition of an authorisation.) Section 3.3 gave general advice for setting up ambient quality monitoring programmes.

Annual mean concentrations are generally sufficient for assessing the ambient concentration of a substance in air for an IPC application. This means that you do not need high resolution data and can use relatively cheap air sampling methods, rather than expensive continuous automatic monitoring equipment. For example, for sulphur dioxide and nitrogen dioxide you can use passive samplers or diffusion tubes. For organic compounds, a series of bag or canister samples may give you acceptable precision. Six months' measurement would be adequate to give a reliable annual average value provided the six-month period includes both winter (October to March) and summer (April to September) months.

If high resolution data, such as hourly mean concentrations, were required you would have to arrange a monitoring programme for an extended period to obtain a representative spread of values. For example, to obtain a reliable value for the 99th percentile of hourly mean concentrations, you would need to monitor for 3 years to ensure that a full range of meteorological conditions had occurred. This is not a practical proposition for a typical IPC application. A much shorter period of three to six months may be acceptable providing the data are carefully reviewed and compared to meteorological conditions and measurements at national monitoring network sites.

As far as possible, monitoring points should be sited where people are most likely to be exposed to the highest concentrations expected from the planned new process. In any case, monitoring sites should be agreed with the Environment Agency.

3.5 Ambient water quality

General considerations

Planned releases of water borne effluents from industrial processes reach surface waters by one of two authorised routes:

- As direct discharges to rivers, estuaries or coastal waters; occasionally to canals or lakes.
- As trade effluent discharged to the sewerage system for subsequent treatment in a sewage treatment works with domestic sewage and other trade effluent before discharge to river, estuary or coastal water.

The guidance in this section concentrates on direct discharges and the need for ambient water quality data to assess the impact of direct discharges from processes requiring IPC authorisation.

Discharges from sewage treatment works are also regulated by the Environment Agency, but under the Water Resources Act 1991. An IPC authorisation may include limits on the amounts of hazardous substances in the process effluent discharging to sewer but the process operator is not required to assess any impact that the process effluent might have on the water course that receives the treated effluent from the sewage treatment plant. That is a matter for the company that operates the treatment plant (the sewerage undertaker) and the Environment Agency. The trade effluent consent serves two purposes:

● it specifies the quantity and quality of the trade effluent that will be the basis of the charges paid by the discharger to the sewerage undertaker for providing the effluent removal and treatment service;

● it is a statutory authorisation from the sewerage undertaker setting limits on the quantity and composition the trade effluent. In this the sewerage undertaker is acting as a regulator under the Water Industry Act, 1991.

In this guidance, ambient water quality means the existing concentrations of substances in surface water. Unlike the atmosphere, where pollutants mix and disperse in all directions, bodies of water have well defined boundaries and flow patterns. Consequently it is seldom possible to make reliable estimates of ambient water quality at one location by making comparisons or extrapolations from measurements made at another location. Fortunately there is a great deal of information on concentrations of substances in most of the surface waters in the UK. For this reason the guidance concentrates on obtaining ambient quality information for the actual surface water that is receiving a discharge from the process.

Another important difference between ambient air quality information and water quality data is that the question of measurement resolution is much simpler. While there are considerable short-term variations in concentrations of substances in rivers, as flows rise and fall with rainfall, continuous monitoring for short-term values is not done to anything like the extent it is for air quality. This is partly a question of cost but primarily because air quality impacts directly on human health whereas water can be purified before being used as drinking water. Water quality management focuses on improving the long-term average quality of surface waters to benefit aquatic species. Most of the monitoring is based on regular spot or composite samples to provide long-term average concentrations.

The Environment Agency also uses biological assay methods for assessing the quality of surface waters and the impact of individual discharges. Methods for toxicity based assessment are also being developed. These measures are not usually considered for IPC applications at the present time. The guidance in this section concentrates on ambient quality in terms of concentrations of individual substances, or types of substances, in surface waters.

A structured approach for assessing ambient water quality

Figure 3.9 shows a series of steps that you can follow to make the most appropriate estimates of ambient water quality for assessing the effects of substances discharged to surface waters.

The following notes explain how to the use the procedure in Figure 3.9

NOTE 1

The discharge of an effluent may be direct from the process or via an effluent treatment plant, which in turn may serve more than one IPC process.

The information you have compiled for each release situation (Chapter 2, section 2.2) and the dispersion estimates for significant releases should have identified the type of receiving water and the likely extent of measurable contamination. The type of receiving water - river or estuary or coastal water - affects the particular characteristics of ambient quality data that you will need (see NOTE 4).

NOTE 2

Many processes discharge to sewer, with or without some form of on-site treatment, rather than directly to a watercourse. As the process operator, you are not required to assess any impact that your effluent might have on the watercourse that receives the treated effluent from the sewage treatment plant. Therefore, you do not need to investigate the ambient quality of the water receiving the sewage work's discharge.

NOTE 3

If the PC is less than 2% of the EQC, or if the substance released is unlikely to be present in the surface water, you will not need to establish ambient quality data.

Figure 3.9 Steps for the assessment of ambient water quality

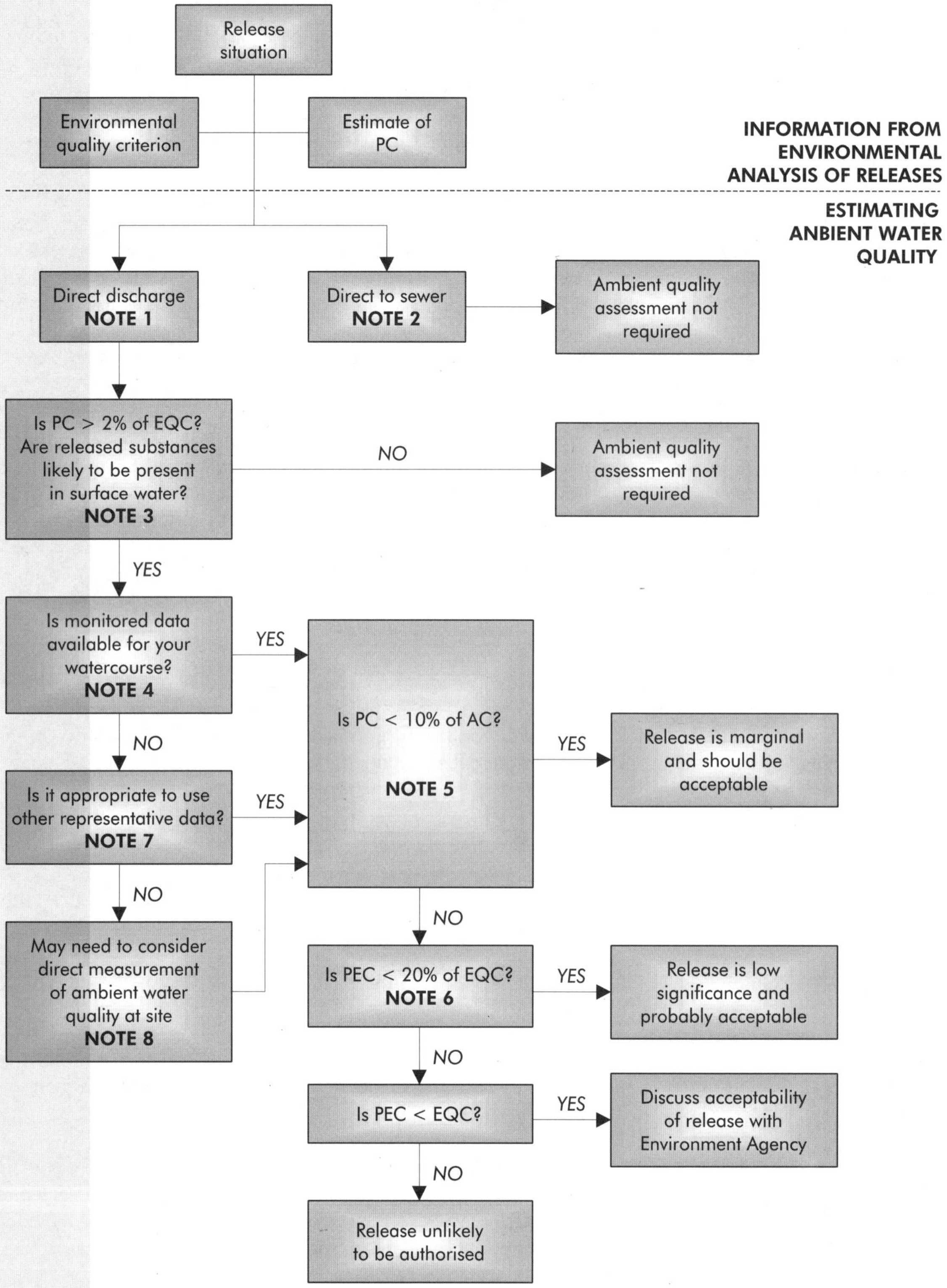

Appendix 2.3(c) gives lists of statutory and advisory EQCs for substances in surface waters.

Your new process may plan to discharge substances for which there are currently no published EQCs. The first step is to find out if the substances are likely to cause environmental harm. The Environment Agency's National Centre for Ecotoxicology and Hazardous Substances (EHS) (Tel: 01491 828544) may be able to provide a tentative EQC or Predicted No Effect Concentration (PNEC), which can be used as an EQC, to assess whether the amounts discharged are likely to be significant and whether ambient quality data is needed. Another source of this type of information is the National Centre for Environmental Toxicology, run by the Water Research Centre (WRc) (Tel: 01491 571531).

NOTE 4

Information on surface water quality is available for all major rivers and estuaries. The primary sources of monitoring data for the water environment are the Public Registers available at local Environment Agency offices. The amount of information varies between locations with more data available for rivers and relatively less for coastal waters. The Agency's web site at http://www.environment-agency.gov.uk gives a list of the types of information held in the registers.

This means that in many cases you will be able to use measured ambient data for the AC in the watercourse that will receive your new effluent. If the new process is an addition or modification to an existing process, which is already discharging the same substances, you should add the existing process contributions to ambient concentrations from a monitoring site upstream of the process to give the AC for the new process.

You should check that the monitoring point used for determining AC is representative of the water quality at the site of your proposed discharge. If there are any other discharges between the monitoring point and your new discharge, or adjacent land uses which are likely to produce contaminated run-off, their contribution should be taken into account. Wherever possible, look at monitoring data upstream and downstream to gauge the impact of existing activities on the quality of the watercourse.

Water quality monitoring sites are set up for various purposes and the data they provide varies accordingly.

Environment Agency monitoring points for classifying water quality includes:

- Monitoring to check compliance with statutory requirement;
- Investigative monitoring, such as discharge impact studies.

As well as Environment Agency monitoring data, other sources of water quality data are:

- Scottish Environmental Protection Agency (SEPA) - similar monitoring programme to the Environment Agency, but for Scotland.
- DoE(NI) Environment & Heritage Service - similar monitoring programme to the Environment Agency, but for Northern Ireland.
- DETR - Harmonised Monitoring Scheme - 115 physical, chemical and microbiological determinands. Over 20 years data for 209 sites nationally.
- Centre for Environment, Fisheries and Aquaculture Science (CEFAS) - primarily coastal waters. Physical, chemical, biological, water column, sediment and radioactivity data.

The question of data resolution is not as complicated for water as it is for air. Water quality criteria are mostly defined as annual averages, 95th percentiles or maximum concentrations. Monitoring is usually in the form of discrete samples taken at a defined frequency, such as monthly, for laboratory analysis. The results are used to calculate the concentration at the required resolution. The raw data and statistics for the relevant resolution are available from the Environment Agency.

NOTE 5

The Environment Agency's policy on applications for consent for new discharges is that there should be no "significant deterioration" in the quality of the receiving water. This policy is set out in Chapter 2 of the Agency's Discharge Consents Manual (Ref. 11). The relevant points are:

- For rivers: "no planned change of more than 10% in the mean and 90th percentile concentrations of key determinands in the receiving water as recorded in 1990 unless there is insignificant environment change as a consequence;"
- For estuaries and coastal waters: "For all discharges, no planned change of more than 10% in receiving water quality of key determinands, unless there is insignificant environmental change as a consequence. (For coastal discharges, particular regard should be paid to bacteriological parameters in relevant circumstances)."

This means that if the PC of a particular substance is not more than 10% of the AC, it may be regarded as *trivial*.

If your proposed discharge is estimated to cause more than a 10% increase on ambient concentration, you would need to show that there would be "insignificant environmental changes as a consequence". This assessment is usually made by comparing the PEC with the EQC. If the PEC is less than 20% of the EQC, then the release would generally be accepted as being of low significance.

For the majority of new discharges the data sources given in Note 4 will indicate monitoring sites that provide reliable data for assessing the AC. However, if your new discharge is at a location for which there are no relevant monitoring sites, you would then have to consider whether a reliable estimate of AC could be based on typical UK data. The problem with attempting this approach for water is that each watercourse is uniquely affected by the activities in its own catchment area and extrapolation from one to another is generally not reliable. (This is in contrast to the usefulness of this approach for estimating ambient air quality.)

The best you could do is to identify any other watercourses that have similar characteristics in terms of flow, geology and land uses in their catchment areas. You may be able to identify a monitoring point used for routine Environment Agency monitoring or for the DETR Harmonised Monitoring Scheme which is similar to the location of your proposed discharge. You could then use that monitoring point data as your estimate for AC. As far as possible, make allowance for any local pollution sources that are different from the representative monitoring site. Before you use this approach in support of an IPC or discharge consent application, contact the Environment Agency to agree the values of AC.

If none of the previous methods of estimating AC are available and the PC of a substance to be discharged is likely to be more than 10% of the EQC, you may have to undertake a local monitoring programme to obtain reliable ambient quality data. You should plan such a programme with the Environment Agency. The Environment Agency has produced a 'Manual of Best Practice for the Design of Water Quality Monitoring Programmes' (Ref. 12). This gives guidance for designing a monitoring programme. It includes a set of software tools to aid in the planning and data analysis process.

3.6   Ambient land quality

General considerations

Wastes from your IPC processes may end up on or in land in a number of ways:

1. Transfers to a land based waste disposal facility, e,g, a landfill site. The requirements of IPC authorisation for the process producing the wastes are simply to show that all stages of the disposal route are properly licensed to handle the type of waste. The transfer and disposal activities are regulated by the Environment Agency under Part II of the Environmental Protection Act 1990 and consequent Regulations. Under this legislation the waste producer, the carrier and the waste disposer have "duty of care" responsibilities but the waste producer is not required to assess the environmental impacts of the final waste disposal process. As the IPC process operator you do not, therefore, have to make an assessment of the environmental effects of the disposal process.

    This type of release to land is not considered further in this guidance.

2. Direct releases of waste substances to land that may be authorised from IPC process are either:

(a) controlled spreading onto agricultural land as means of waste disposal with soil conditioning benefits,

(b) deposition of gaseous substances or particulate matter which has been released as an airborne emission.

This section provides advice for obtaining information on ambient land quality for assessing the environmental effects of these two categories of releases to land.

3.   An IPC application for a new process must show that appropriate measures are taken to prevent accidental releases that could cause contamination of land and groundwater, but IPC regulation does not cover the management of contaminated land. Regulations for that purpose will be introduced under Part V of the Environment Act, 1995. The implementation of the IPPC Directive from October 1999 will introduce new requirements for plant operators in regard to site restoration.

The guidance in this section does not deal with any aspect of contaminated land management.

Characteristics of "land" for environmental assessment of releases

For the purpose of this guidance, "land" is the area of ground affected by your process. That area may include urban and rural areas and a variety of land uses. The guidance in this section is based on soil quality data, expressed as concentrations of substances in soil. This is the only type of information on "land quality" that can be applied in a general manner. However, it is very much a simplification because "land" is not just soil. Conclusions about the acceptability of a release that affects land, based on soil quality criteria, should always be reviewed against the specific land uses in the area affected by the process.   Some examples of site-specific characteristics that you should take into account are:

- *Urban areas*: are there any particularly sensitive sites such as schools, playgrounds, hospitals, etc. that justify more stringent limits on airborne deposition?

- *Industrial areas*: are there other sources of the same substances that would add to the deposition from your process?

- *Rural areas*: are there any particularly sensitive sites, such as horticulture/market gardens, specialist growers, nature reserves, Sites of Special Scientific Interest (SSSI), etc. that justify more stringent limits on airborne deposition or restrict the use of controlled spreading?

- *Surface waters*: is there likely to be run-off into water that would interfere with its use, e.g. potential contamination of a reservoir used for public water supply?

All the guidance in this book for assessing releases to air and water, by comparing PEC with EQC, is based on the simplifying assumption that the released substances do not degrade in the environment. This is clearly a conservative assumption because most substances degrade to a greater or lesser extent over time through natural chemical or biological processes in the atmosphere or in watercourses. However, for the relatively short time - in the order of minutes rather than hours - that an airborne or waterborne pollutant travels between a release point and the controlling measurement point in the environment, the assumption of no degradation is a reasonable basis for environmental assessment for IPC.

In contrast to air and water, which disperse pollutants relatively rapidly, land is essentially a static medium. Many substances remain in soil for a long time because rates of degradation and dispersion are very slow. Estimates of deposition rates of released substances, in terms of kg/ha/yr or mg/m^2/day, must be converted into estimates of the concentration that will accumulate in the surface layer of soil over a stated time period, such as the expected lifetime of the project. However, because the timescales are now very long - years or tens of years - allowance should also be made for degradation and dispersion, even though these are very slow processes for many substances in soil. The following paragraphs give guidance for making these estimates.

EQCs for soil are generally expressed as maximum concentrations on a weight for weight basis, e,g, mg/kg or ppm, without reference to any timescale or averaging time.

In the general form of environmental assessment, PC + AC = PEC < EQC, PC is the total amount your process will add to the soil, expressed as a concentration in soil, over the stated time period; AC is the existing concentration of the substance in soil in the area under the *process footprint*.

A structured approach for assessing ambient soil quality

Figure 3.11 shows a series of steps that you can follow to make the most appropriate estimate of ambient soil quality for assessing the environmental effect of released substances on land.

Figure 3.10 Steps for estimating ambient soil quality

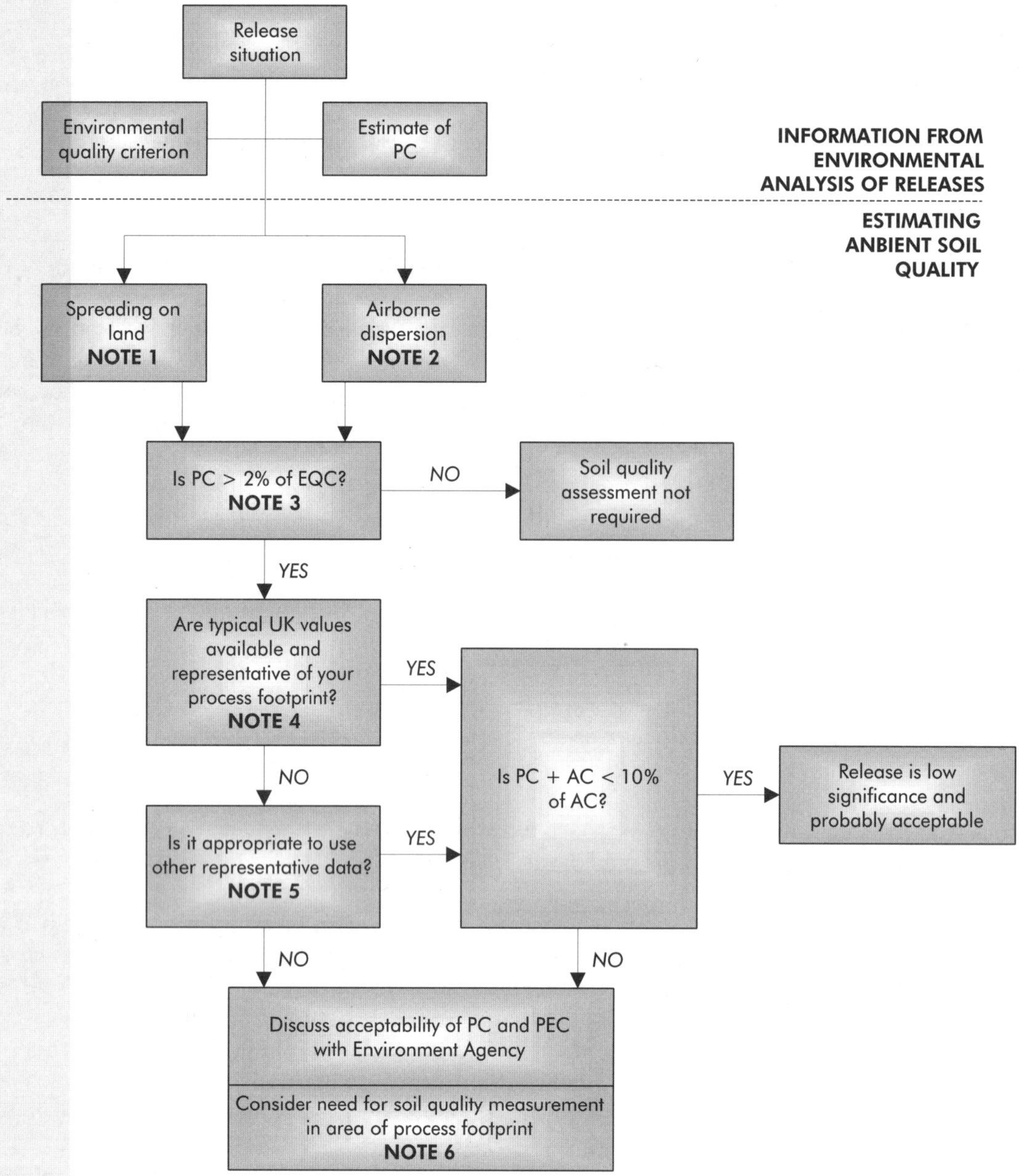

The following notes explain how to use the procedure in Figure 3.10.

NOTE 1

Direct disposal of wastes by spreading on agricultural land is limited to wastes which are beneficial for conditioning the soil and which have low concentrations of potentially harmful substances, such as heavy metals. Regulations governing the disposal of sewage sludge to agricultural land (Ref. 13) include limits for "potentially toxic elements" (PTE) in soil and maximum permissible average annual rates of PTE addition over a 10-year period.   These limits are given in Appendix 2.2(d).

NOTE 2

Deposition from atmospheric emissions is potentially an important environmental effect when the emissions contain heavy metals or persistent and toxic compounds that would accumulate in surface soil. Deposition may also be an important mechanism for substances that can accumulate on vegetation and enter the food chain, such as emissions of fluorides leading to deposition on grassland and subsequent take up by grazing animals.

Dispersion modelling techniques, as described in section 2.3, provide estimates of PC as a pollutant loading, or deposition flux, expressed as mass per unit time per unit area, e.g. $g/s/m^2$. Ambient data for soil is usually in terms of weight for weight e.g. mg/kg, as are soil quality criteria. Therefore, it will be necessary to convert the PC to the same basis for comparison with AC and EQC. Formulae to carry out this conversion are given below.

Persistent pollutants:

For pollutants that remain unchanged when deposited, and are not removed from the soil by chemical processes or leaching, or the rates of degradation and dispersion are very slow, the process contribution to soil quality is given by:

$$PC_{mg/kg} = \frac{f}{d \times \rho} \times T$$

where:
- f = deposition flux of pollutant $(mg/day/m^2)$
- d = mixing depth for pollutant
- ρ = soil density $(1000 \ kg/m^3)$
- T = likely operational time of process (days)

The mixing depth varies with location and type of land surface. Typical depths are 0.075m for pasture to 0.3m for ploughed land. If the mixing depth is unknown, use the conservative value of 0.075m.

Degradable pollutants:

The above formula does not allow for any degradation or migration of substances in soil. The following formula includes a decay term.

$$PC_{mg/kg} = \frac{f}{kd\rho}$$

where:
- f = deposition flux of pollutant $(mg/day/m^2)$
- d = mixing depth for pollutant (see above)
- ρ = soil density $(1000 \ kg/m^3)$
- k = $\dfrac{\ln 2}{t_{0.5}}$ where $t_{0.5}$ = half-life (days)

This formula assumes that equilibrium is reached between the rate of deposition and the rate of removal of the substance. This is valid if the duration of the release, i.e. life of the process causing the release, is at least ten times the half-life of the substance in soil.

Appendix 3.6(a) gives more information about the fate of substances in soil and half-life data for a selection of substances

NOTE 3

Ambient quality data is not normally needed if the PC is less than 2% of the EQC. Appendix 2.3(d) gives EQCs for inorganic elements in soil. The values are taken from regulations governing the disposal of sewage sludge to land, but can be used as general quality criteria for controlling contamination of soil.

NOTE 4

Typical UK background data can be obtained from the following sources:

- 'The Soil Geochemical Atlas of England and Wales', 1992 (Ref. 14)
- 'Heavy Metals in Soils', 1990 (Ref. 15)
- 'Soils in the Urban Environment', 1991 (Ref. 16)
- 'Metal Contamination in British Urban Dusts and Soils', 1988 (Ref. 17)
- 'Baseline Survey of Metals in Welsh Soils', 1985 (Ref. 18)

Most of the data is for metals in soil, such as lead, copper, chromium etc. Figures 3.12, 3.13 and 3.14 give some typical data derived from the above references to indicate the orders of magnitude of metals in soils.

The data in these references will often be sufficient to give you an indication of whether your process is likely to add significantly to the soil pollution burden in your area. For example, the regional data might show that the mean total copper content of soils in your area is 100 mg/kg, but your process might only be expected to add 1 mg/kg to this burden over a 5 year period (assuming no dispersion through the soil). This level of assessment should be sufficient to show that your release would not significantly affect local soil quality.

Figure 3.11 Concentrations (mg/kg) of some common elements in top soil in England and Wales (Ref. 12)

Element	Minimum	25th %ile	50th %ile	75th %ile	Maximum
Cadmium	< 0.2	0.5	0.7	1.0	47.9
Chromium	0.2	26.5	39.3	52.6	837.8
Copper	1.2	12.6	18.1	24.9	1507.7
Lead	3	28	40	66	16338
Nickel	0.8	14.0	22.6	32.4	439.5
Zinc	5	59	82	108	3648

Figure 3.12 Baseline survey of metals in Welsh soils, mg/kg (Ref. 16)

Species/Soil horizon		Minimum	Median	Maximum
PH	Top Soil	2.0	4.4	7.8
	Sub Soil	2.3	4.0	7.0
Lead	Top Soil	1.3	35	3370
	Sub Soil	0.2	17	2100
Zinc	Top Soil	4.7	63	2120
	Sub Soil	0.04	59	1450
Copper	Top Soil	0.13	12	214
	Sub Soil	0.09	11	65
Cadmium	Top Soil	0.01	0.29	15
	Sub Soil	0.01	0.12	12
Nickel	Top Soil	0.42	14	169
	Sub Soil	0.63	19	79

Figure 3.13 Metal contamination in British urban dusts and soils, mg/kg (Sample population = 100) (Ref. 15)

Sample Type	Lead	Cadmium	Zinc	Copper
Garden soil				
Geometric Mean	6.9	1.2	278	56
Range	< 1 - 8040	< 1 - 40	13 - 14600	5 - 16800
Vegetable plot soil				
Geometric Mean	270	1.2	321	56
Range	24 - 2560	< 1 - 9	41 - 2780	8 - 487
Public garden soil				
Geometric Mean	185	1.2	180	46
Range	20 - 1820	<1 - 11	34 - 1360	8 - 1400

NOTE 5

Representative data on soil quality in a given locality is likely to be very limited, although an increasing amount of soil quality measurement is taking place for contaminated land management and for new developments on brownfield sites. Contact the Local Authority and the Environment Agency to see if they have any data or reports specific to your area.

NOTE 6

It is extremely unlikely that new measurements of local soil quality would be required for preparing an IPC application for a process with airborne releases that cause deposition on land. For new processes the use of modern abatement technology that would be accepted as BATNEEC should limit particulate releases to low concentrations of very fine particles with consequently low deposition rates. However the question of new measurement of soil quality may arise if there is a history of local contamination or concerns over sensitive sites within the process footprint.

Any programme of sampling and analysis should be planned with the local Environment Agency.

References

6. UK National Air Quality Archive, available on
    http://www.aeat.co.uk/netcn/aqarchive/archome.html
7. DETR & NETCEN. Air Pollution in the UK. (published annually). Available from NETCEN, Culham Science and Engineering Centre, Abingdon, OX14 3DB.
8. DETR. Digest of Environmental Statistics. The Stationary Office. (published annually).
9. Meteorological Office and DETR. (June 1995) A-Z Air Pollution. Available from Atmospheric process Research Branch, The Met. Office, Bracknell.
10. Loader A., Willis P. and Broughton G (1998) Investigation into the use of surrogate statistics for Local Authority air quality review and asessment. RAMP 20440004. Culham: AEA Technology. Available from NETCEN, Culham Science and Engineering Centre, Abingdon, OX14 3DB.
11. Environment Agency (November 1997) Discharge Control Manual
12. Environment Agency (1998) Manual if Best Practice for the Design of Water Quality Monitoring Programmes (in preparation).
13. Sludge (Use in Agriculture) Regulations 1989 (SI 1989, No. 1263). Also DoE (1989) Code of Practice for Agriculture Use of Sewage Sludge.
14. McGrath, S.P. & Loveland, P.J. (1992). The Soil Geochemical Atlas of England and Wales. Blackie Academic, Glasgow.
15. Alloway, B.J.(ed) (1990) Heavy metals in Soils. Blackie Academic, Glasgow
16. Bullock, P., Gregory, P.J. (eds) (1991) Soils in the Urban Environment. Blackie Academic, Glasgow.
17. Culbard, E.B., Thornton, I., Watt, J., Wheatley, M., Moorcroft, S. & Thompson, M. (1988) Metal Contamination in British Urban Dusts and Soils. Journal of Environmental Quality 17, 226-234.
18. Davies, B.E. (1985) Baseline Survey of Metals in Welsh Soils. Proc. of 1st International Symposium on Geochemistry and Health.

Chapter 4   Worked Example

4.1   Introduction

In this chapter we use data from a manufacturing process to illustrate how the techniques we have recommended for assessing releases can be applied to a project. The proposed process that we will examine has a variety of releases which have been compiled to illustrate most of the assessment techniques described in the previous chapters. The process has two releases to air, containing combustion products and particulates including metallic fume, and a waterborne effluent containing metals.

Figure 4.1 shows the location (imaginary) of the process on a tidal estuary with neighbouring land uses.

Figure 4.1 Site location

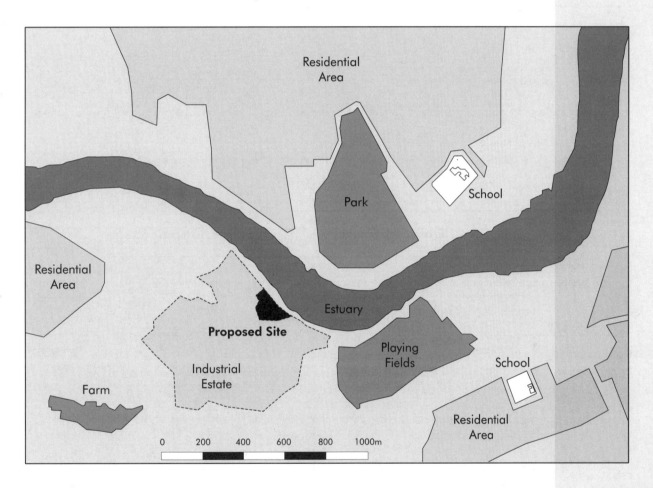

4.2   Emission inventory

The first step is to compile a complete inventory of all the releases from the process. Guidance for doing this is given in chapter 1, section 1.3.

<u>Releases to Air</u>

There are two sources of atmospheric emissions:

- A 50m stack taking combustion products and fumes from gas-fired metallurgical melting operations.
- An 22m extraction vent at the north end of the process building taking the exhausts from refining operations and ventilation systems on casting operations.

Figure 4.2 shows the release characteristics of the two sources.

Figure 4.2 **Characteristics of Releases to Air**

Parameter	From 50m stack	From extraction vent
Actual Flowrate (m³/hr) [a]	500,000 (600,000)	100,000
Height (m)	50	22
Diameter (m)	3.22	1.53
Exit Velocity (m/s)	17 (20)	15
Temperature (K)	333	303

Notes:

(a) Figures in brackets are peak figures which occur for no more than 10% of operating hours.

Figure 4.3 shows the normal and peak concentrations and release rates of substances in the emissions to air.

Figure 4.3 **Atmospheric Emissions – normal and peak concentrations and release rates**

Substance released	From 50m stack				From extraction vent		Total annual release (tonnes)
	Normal concentration (mg/Nm³)	Normal release rate (g/s)	Peak concentration (mg/Nm³)	Peak release rate (g/s)	Normal concentration (mg/Nm³)	Normal release rate (g/s)	
CO_2	25,000	2.846			20,000	518	103,500
CO	5	0.57	100	13.7	20	0.52	73
NOx (as NO_2)	200	22.8	400	54.7	200	5.2	942
SO_2	10	1.14	10	1.37	15	0.39	47
Particulates	10	1.14	50	6.85	15	0.39	64
Cadmium	0.01	0.0011	0.05	0.0068	0.02	0.0005	0.066
Chromium	0.01	0.0011	0.02	0.0027	0.02	0.0005	0.053
Copper	0.05	0.0057	0.10	0.0137	0.05	0.0013	0.236
Lead	0.4	0.0455	0.5	0.0683	0.4	0.0103	1.76
Nickel	0.08	0.0091	0.10	0.0137	0.08	0.0021	0.353
Zinc	0.4	0.0455	0.5	0.0683	0.4	0.0103	1.76

Releases to Water

All the process sources of aqueous effluent are combined for on-site treatment before discharge to the estuary. The concentrations and release rates of metals are given in Figure 4.4. The pH and the temperature of the effluent are also shown. The effluent is discharged continuously at a rate of 36 m³/hr.

Figure 4.4 Releases to Water

Release (or effluent property)	Effluent Concentration (µg/l)	Release Rate (g/s)	Annual Release rate (T/yr)
Cadmium	130	0.0013	0.038
Chromium	800	0.008	0.235
Iron	100	0.001	0.029
Lead	100	0.001	0.029
Zinc	2300	0.023	0.676
PH	8		
Temperature (°C)	+ 1	The temperature of the discharge is 1°C higher than the water extracted for cooling	

Releases to Land

The only release to land is airborne deposition from the particulate emissions to air that contain metals. The release rates of metals to air are shown in Figure 4.3.

4.3   Release situations

We show the procedure for identifying release situations with one example each of an emission to air (prefixed "A"), a discharge to water (prefixed "W") and airborne deposition to land (prefixed "L"). For each environmental compartment we then give a tabular summary of the release situations that we will assess.

Releases to Air

Figure 4.5 shows the release situation for airborne emissions of lead from both sources, following the procedure described in section 2.2.

Figure 4.5 Example of a Release Situation for airborne releases

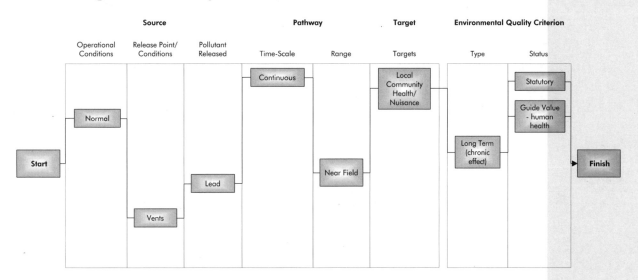

Figure 4.6 summarises all the release situations that we have identified in this way. It includes the short term peak-rate releases for those substances that have short term EQCs for guarding against acute health effects, e.g. CO, NO_2, SO_2 and PM_{10}. Short term peak emissions of metals are not considered separately because

EQCs for metals in air are based on long term chronic effects. We base our assessment of airborne metal releases on the total amounts released, including 10% of operating time at the peak release rates shown in Figure 4.3.

Figure 4.6 Release situations for airborne releases

Release Situation	Operational Mode	Substance	EQC
A1	Normal	CO_2	No concentration standard
A2	Peak	CO	WHO health guideline - 1 hour mean
A3	Peak	NO_2	NAQS target - 1 hour mean
A4	Normal	NO_2	NAQS target - annual mean
A5	Peak	SO_2	NAQS target - 15 min. mean
A6	Normal	SO_2	EU Directive - annual mean
A7	Peak	PM_{10}	NAQS target - 24 hour mean
A8	Normal	PM_{10}	NAQS target - annual mean
A9	Normal	Cadmium	WHO guide value - annual mean
A10	Normal	Chromium	EAL based on OEL - annual mean [a]
A11	Normal	Copper	EAL based on OEL - annual mean [a]
A12 (b)	Normal	Lead	NAQS target - annual mean
A13	Normal	Nickel	EAL based on OEL - annual mean [a]
A14	Normal	Zinc	EAL based on OEL - annual mean [a]

Note:

(a) Very few air quality criteria have been developed for metallic elements. The Environment Agency has proposed Environmental Assessment Levels (EAL) that are based on the Occupational Exposure Limits (OEL) used by the Health & Safety Executive for occupational health protection.

(b) This is the release situation shown in Figure 4.5.

Releases to Water

Figure 4.7 shows the release situations for discharges of heavy metals to the estuary during normal operation.

Figure 4.7 Example of a release situation for a water borne release

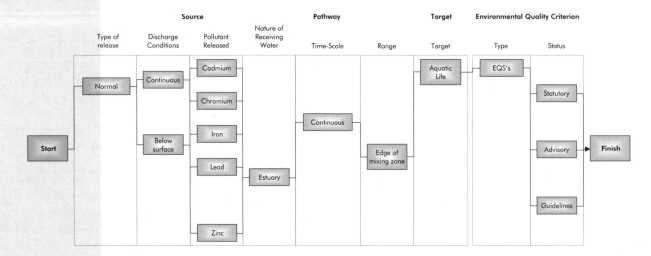

Low concentrations of metals are discharged to the estuary on a continuous basis during normal operation. Short term discharges of higher concentrations of metals are not considered here. They are extremely unlikely because of the hold up capacity in the effluent treatment plant. Moreover EQCs for metals in water are based on chronic effects due to accumulation in sediments and bio-accumulation in aquatic food chains.

Figure 4.8 summarises the release situations for discharges to water.

Figure 4.8 Release situations for discharges to water

Release situation	Operational Mode	Substance	EQC
W1	Normal	Cadmium	EQS
W2	Normal	Chromium	EQS
W3	Normal	Iron	EQS
W4	Normal	Lead	EQS
W5	Normal	Zinc	EQS

Releases to Land

The only releases to land are airborne deposition from particulate emissions to air. The release situations are therefore similar to those for airborne releases, as shown in Figure 4.9 for cadmium releases.

Figure 4.9 Example of a release situation for airborne deposition to land

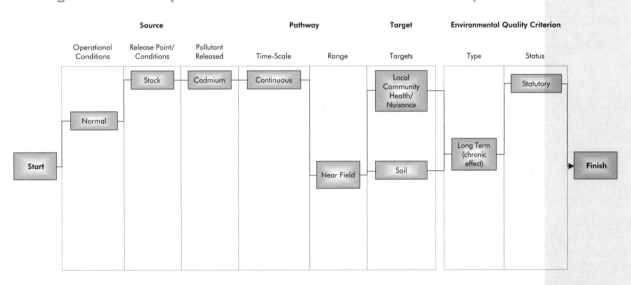

The release situations for airborne depositions to land are summarised in Figure 4.10. Assessment will be based on the total amounts of metals released over a year because the EQCs for metals in soil are based on long term accumulative effects.

Figure 4.10 Release situations for airborne deposition to land

Release situation	Operational Mode	Substance	EQC
L1	Normal	Cadmium	DoE Max Permissible Concentration
L2	Normal	Chromium	DoE Max Permissible Concentration
L3	Normal	Copper	DoE Max Permissible Concentration
L4	Normal	Lead	DoE Max Permissible Concentration
L5	Normal	Nickel	DoE Max Permissible Concentration
L6	Normal	Zinc	DoE Max Permissible Concentration

4.4 Selection of EQCs

In the release situations that we have identified in Figures 4.6, 4.8 and 4.10 we have shown the relevant EQC for each release. These are based on the following considerations:

- Use a statutory environmental quality standard (EQS) where that is available.
- If there is no relevant EQS, use a published guide value from an authoritative source.
- If neither of the above is available consider using a value derived from other related sources, e.g. occupational exposure levels (OEL) for substances in air or reputable sources of toxicological or eco-toxicological data.
- The EQC should be relevant for the most sensitive receptors in the release situation.
- The EQC should be relevant to the potential environmental effects of the released substance, e.g. maximum allowable concentration or short term value for acute effects; a long term value for chronic effects.

Appendices 2.3(a), 2.3(c) and 2.3(d) give environmental quality criteria for substances in air, water and soil respectively.

For carbon dioxide there are no EQC values as such because the environmental effect of concern is climate change due to long term accumulation of CO_2 in the global atmosphere, not the concentration at ground level. We can assess the significance of the process emission of CO_2 by comparing it with the UK total emission. This is explained in the next section.

Figure 4.11 shows the EQCs we have selected for substances emitted to air in the release situations identified in Figure 4.6.

Figure 4.11 EQCs for substances in air

Substance	Type of EQC	Source	EQC Value (mg/m³)	Temporal Basis[b] or Resolution
CO	Short term	WHO Health Guideline	30	1-hour mean
NO_2 [a]	Short term	NAQS target	0.200	1-hour mean
NO_2 [a]	Long term	NAQS target	0.04	Annual mean
SO_2	Short term	NAQS target	0.350	1-hour mean
SO_2	Long term	EU Directive	0.08	Annual mean (median of daily values)
PM_{10}	Short term	NAQS target	0.05	24-hour mean
PM_{10}	Long term	NAQS target	0.03	Annual mean
Cadmium	Long term	WHO guide value	5 E-06	Annual mean
Chromium	Long term	EAL based on OEL	0.0001	Annual mean
Copper	Long term	EAL based on OEL	0.01	Annual mean
Lead	Long term	NAQS target	0.0005	Annual mean
Nickel	Long term	EAL based on OEL	0.01	Annual mean
Zinc	Long term	EAL based on OEL	0.05	Annual mean

Notes:

(a) For some processes, releases of oxides of nitrogen (NOx) are quoted, instead of an equivalent value in terms of NO_2, as in this example. For combustion processes much of the NOx is nitric oxide, NO. To some extent released NO is converted to NO_2 in the atmosphere but not entirely. Using the NO_2

equivalent represents a conservative approach for assessing these releases.

(b) It is important that PCs and PECs are expressed at the same resolution as the EQC for comparisons to be valid (see section 3.3).

Figure 4.12 shows the EQCs we have selected for the substances released to water. All the released substances in this example have statutory EQSs.

Figure 4.12 EQCs for substances in water

Substance	Source	EQC (µg/l)	Temporal Basis
Cadmium	Surface Waters (Dangerous Substances) (Classification) Regulations	5	Annual mean
Chromium	Circular 7/89 (DoE, 1989)	15	Annual mean
Iron	Circular 7/89 (DoE, 1989)	1000	Annual mean
Lead	Circular 7/89 (DoE, 1989)	25	Annual mean
Zinc	Circular 7/89 (DoE, 1989)	40	Annual mean

Figure 4.13 shows the EQCs for metals in soils. The values represent the maximum permissible concentration of metals in soil on agricultural land. For zinc, copper and nickel the permitted concentration depends on the pH of the soil. For other metals a single value applies provided the soil pH is 5.0 or above. There is no similar standard for iron in soil. If airborne deposition of iron had been a feature of our plant we would assess its significance in relation to typical iron levels in soil.

Figure 4.13 EQCs for substances in soil

Substance	Permitted Range (mg/kg)	Selected EQC (mg/kg)
Cadmium	3	3
Chromium	400	400
Copper	80-200	100
Lead	300	300
Nickel	50-110	60
Zinc	200-450	250

4.5   Assessing significance of the releases

The procedure for assessing the significance of releases is summarised in Figure 2.14 in section 2.4. It can be split into 3 distinct stages:

1. Comparison of RC with EQC
2. Comparison of PC with EQC
3. Comparison of PEC with EQC

This sequence provides the most cost-effective way of screening the releases for their significance. We use the most readily available information first and thereby minimise the need for more complex analysis. Data on the RC of each release is already available in the emission inventory; estimation of PC requires use of a simple dispersion model (as described in section 2.3) and estimation of PEC requires PC plus estimation of AC (as described in Chapter 3). Releases that can be screened out as trivial on the basis of RC at stage 1 do not then require estimation of PC; releases that are screened out as trivial on the basis of PC at stage 2 do not require estimation of PEC.

We now use this procedure to assess the triviality and significance of the releases to air.

Stage 1: Comparing RC with EQC

The table in Figure 4.14 shows the RCs for the releases to air. We have taken a conservative approach by taking the highest value of RC from the two release points for each substance (taken from Figure 4.3 for the release situations identified in Figure 4.6) and used these values as the RCs for comparison with the relevant EQCs from Figure 4.11. If these comparisons show that the release of a substance is trivial we can be confident that the other releases of that substance are also trivial on this criterion.

Figure 4.14 Comparison of RC and EQC for emissions to air

Release Situation	Substance	Temporal Basis	RC (mg/m³)	EQC (mg/m³)	RC/EQC	Environmental Effect
A2	CO	Short term	100	30	3	Trivial
A3	NO_2	Short term	400	0.2	2000	Potentially significant
A4	NO_2	Long term	200	0.04	5000	Potentially significant
A5	SO_2	Short term	10	0.350	29	Trivial
A6	SO_2	Long term	15	0.08	188	Potentially significant
A7	PM_{10}	Short term	50	0.05	1000	Potentially significant
A8	PM_{10}	Long term	10	0.03	333	Potentially significant
A9	Cadmium	Long term	0.014	5.0 E-06	2800	Potentially significant
A10	Chromium	Long term	0.011	0.0001	110	Potentially significant
A11	Copper	Long term	0.055	0.01	6	Trivial
A12	Lead	Long term	0.41	0.0005	820	Potentially significant
A14	Nickel	Long term	0.082	0.01	8	Trivial
A15	Zinc	Long term	1.2	0.05	24	Trivial

If the ratio RC/EQC is less than 50, then the release can be regarded as trivial. *If RC/EQC is greater than 50, then it is necessary to proceed to the next stage of the assessment and compare the PC with the EQC, as the release could be significant. On this basis the short term CO and SO_2 and the long term copper, nickel and zinc releases can be regarded as trivial because the RC is less than 50 times the EQC. For the other releases, further assessment is required to determine significance or triviality.*

For CO_2, there are no EQCs as concentrations in air because CO_2 is a naturally occurring (and essential) component of the atmosphere. The concern about CO_2 is that fossil fuel burning is raising the natural background concentrations to levels that may be causing global warming. International negotiations are likely to lead to national programmes for reducing CO_2 emissions so it is prudent to assess the contribution our process is making to the UK national total. Since the environmental effect of CO_2 is related to total mass emitted, we compare the annual release of CO_2 from the process with total UK emissions. The Digest of Environmental Statistics produced by the DETR gives the UK total emission of CO_2 in 1995 as 572 million tonnes. We can then make the following comparison:

- Annual CO_2 emissions from process: 103,500 tonnes/year
- Total UK CO_2 emissions: 572 million tonnes/year
- Therefore process emission is 0.018 % of UK total emission.

On this basis our plant is a minor source of CO_2 on a national scale but it would still be a requirement of good environmental management practice to show that our process was using energy as efficiently as possible.

Stage 2: Comparing PC with EQC

The next stage of assessment is to estimate the PC for those releases that have not been screened out as trivial in Stage 1. This involves using the guidance in section 2.3 to identify and apply an appropriate method for estimating dispersion of the releases.

Reference RS 1 (Appendix 2.4(a)) provides formulae and nomograms that can be used to estimate the rise of a plume due to its thermal buoyancy. Using the data from Figure 4.2, we find that the thermal rise for the 50 m stack is 30m under normal operating conditions and 33m under peak load conditions. The thermal rise for the 22m extraction vent is 7m. We will therefore use effective heights of 80m for the main stack and 29m for the extraction vent to estimate the ground level concentrations of released substances.

Release situation A3 - short term peak emissions of NO_2

Reference RS 3 (Appendix 2.4(c)) provides nomograms that can be used for estimating the ground level concentrations for short term (30 minute) releases. From Figure 16 of RS 3, we find that the maximum time integrated concentration for a short duration release from 80m discharge height is 3×10^{-6} g sec m^{-3}. We then adjust this for a release duration of one hour (for comparison with the EQC as a one hour mean value) by using a modifying factor of 0.85 from Figure 23 of RS 3. The maximum ground level concentration (the PC) we can expect from the peak rate of release of NO_2 is: $3 \times 10^{-6} \times 0.85 \times 54.7 \times 10^6$ = 139 μg m^{-3}. This will occur at around 1200m from the stack.

Release situation A4 - long term emissions of NO_2

For continuous releases we will take as the most frequent UK weather conditions the 60% D contour of the UK Pasquill stability map given in RS 3 (Appendix 2.4(c)) and we will use the nomogram in Figure 36 from that reference to estimate the maximum ground level concentration (the PC) of NO_2 due to the normal release rates from both sources.

For the main stack, with an effective discharge height of 80m, the nomogram gives a maximum ground level time integrated concentration of 6×10^{-8} g sec m^{-3}. The normal release rate of NO_2 from the main stack is 22.8 g/sec. This gives a maximum ground level concentration $6 \times 10^{-8} \times 22.8 \times 10^6$ = 1.4 μg m^{-3}. This occurs at about 800 metres from the stack.

For the extraction vent, with an effective discharge height of 29m, the nomogram gives a maximum ground level time integrated concentration of 1×10^{-6} g sec m^{-3}. The release rate of NO_2 from the extraction vent is 5.2 g/sec. This gives a maximum ground level concentration of $1 \times 10^{-6} \times 5.2 \times 10^6$ = 5.2 μg m^{-3}. This occurs at about 200m from the vent.

The two ground level maxima are well separated but, at this screening stage, we will take the conservative approach of assuming overlap for comparison with the EQC. This gives us a PC for NO_2 of 6.6 μg m^{-3}.

Release situations A6, A7, A8, A9, A10, A12

We followed the same procedure, that we used above for the NO_2 emission, to calculate maximum ground level concentrations for all the other releases identified as "potentially significant" in Figure 4.14. The results are given as the PC values in Figure 4.15, where they are compared with the relevant EQC value.

Figure 4.15 Comparison of PC and EQC

Release situation	Substance	Temporal Basis	PC (μg/m³)	EQC (μg/m³)	PC/EQC	Environmental Effect
A3	NO_2	Short term	139	200	0.7	Potentially significant
A4	NO_2	Long term	6.6	40	0.16	Potentially significant
A6	SO_2	Long term	0.46	80	0.006	Marginal
A7	PM_{10}	Short term	17.5	50	0.36	Potentially significant
A8	PM_{10}	Long term	0.46	30	0.015	Marginal
A9	Cadmium	Long term	0.0006	0.005	0.12	Potentially significant
A10	Chromium	Long term	0.0006	0.1	0.006	Marginal
A12	Lead	Long term	0.013	0.5	0.026	Potentially significant

Using the environmental threshold criteria given in section 2.14, a value of PC/EQC below 0.002 indicates that a release may be regarded as trivial. If the PC/EQC value is less than 0.02 the release is considered marginal and in most circumstances is most likely trivial. Applying these criteria to the release situations in Figure 4.15, we find that the normal (long term) release of SO_2, PM_{10} and chromium can be screened out at this stage as marginal, likely to be trivial. Further assessment is required for the other releases to determine their level of significance.

Sensitive Sites

Although not part of this example, it is important to be aware of potentially sensitive sites in the surrounding area, which might include:

- Schools, hospitals, residential areas etc.
- Sensitive habitats such as SSSIs, national parks, nature reserves, special areas of conservation under the Habitats Directive etc.
- Sensitive water bodies such as public supplies, bathing and leisure waters etc.

These may influence the level of detail required in assessing ambient quality.

Stage 3: Comparing PEC with EQC

The releases that have not been screened out before this third and final stage are significant. We must now estimate the PECs of these releases and compare the values with the relevant EQC to determine how significant they are. We estimate the PEC by adding the PC to the concentration of the substance that is already present in the local environment - the ambient concentration (AC) of the substance.

Chapter 3 gives guidance for determining the ambient quality of the environment around the site of your process. We will use the procedures that are summarised in Figure 3.6 (for ambient air quality), Figure 3.10 (for ambient water quality) and Figure 3.11 (for ambient soil quality) to determine AC, and thereby PEC, values for the significant releases.

Ambient air quality

We now follow the staged procedure from Figure 3.6.

Stage 1: Is AC data required?

We need ambient quality data for the all the releases that we have not screened out as trivial on the basis of PC being less than 2% of EQC. Thus we need ambient quality data for:

Nitrogen dioxide - Particulates - Cadmium - Lead

Stage 2: AC based on typical UK values

We can use typical UK values of ambient quality as an initial screening stage, where the PEC is only likely to be small fraction of the EQC (<10%) and therefore the accuracy of the ambient data is not critical.

Our site is close to built up areas so we will use typical UK values for air quality in a 'major suburban area'. We can derive the following AC values:

- An annual average AC for lead ($0.05\mu g/m^3$) is taken from Figure 3.7.
- Annual averages for NO_2 ($46\mu g/m^3$) and PM_{10} ($20\mu g/m^3$) are estimated from the background concentration maps available on the Internet.
- For the short term peak releases of NO_2, SO_2 and PM_{10} we will use the 90th percentile ACs from Figure 3.7 to combine with short term PCs to calculate PECs. (This is explained in Note 2 to Figure 3.7.) The values (converted from ppb) are $77\mu g/m^3$ for NO_2 and $44\mu g/m^3$ for PM_{10}.
- Typical UK values are not available for the other metallic elements.

Figure 4.16 shows these AC values, the resulting PECs and the values of PEC/EQC.

The table shows that the PEC for the normal long term release of lead is greater than 10% of the EQC. Using the criteria in Figure 3.6, this indicates that this estimate of PEC may not be sufficiently precise to assess the significance of this release and we should seek more reliable and site specific ambient quality data.

The PEC / EQC ratios for NO_2 and PM_{10} are greater than 40% so we definitely need more precise local ambient quality data to assess whether such significant releases would be acceptable at our site.

We must also see what local information is available on ambient quality for cadmium. Our estimate of PC indicates that it is a significant release but there are no UK typical data for estimating the AC.

Stage 3: AC based on locally monitored air quality

We now describe the steps we would take to obtain more reliable local ambient quality data for the releases with Stage 2 PEC estimates greater than 10% of EQC.

NO_2

Long Term
From the NO_2 Diffusion Tube Network reports we identify the nearest site within 40km of the plant. 1996 monthly averages are available (at the time of writing) on the Internet, which can be saved into a spreadsheet format. We calculate the annual average value as the mean of monthly averages, giving a concentration of $21\mu g/m^3$.

Short Term
Diffusion tube measurements are not at a high enough resolution to provide an indication of short term ambient air quality. An automatic ambient monitoring site is located within 40km of the plant, measuring continuous NO_2 concentrations. Hourly average concentrations are provided on the Internet. We can save this data as a spreadsheet and calculate the 90th percentile of hourly values for the last year. The result is $69\mu g/m^3$.

These values are shown at the right hand side of the table in Figure 4.16. These more refined estimates of PEC now indicate that the NO_2 peak release are still likely to exceed the short term EQC. The normal releases of NO_2 are only contributing about 16% to the PEC, but the AC is already more than 50% of the long term EQC.

Particulates

The automatic monitoring station also measures fine particulate matter (PM_{10}). We have copied the data into a spreadsheet and calculated a 90th percentile value of $37\mu g/m^3$ (to combine with short term PC). The resulting PEC shown in Figure 4.16 is 110% of the 24 hour mean EQC value.

Figure 4.16 Ambient Concentrations and Predicted Environmental Concentrations

Substance	Averaging period	EQC ($\mu g/m^3$)	PC ($\mu g/m^3$)	Stage 1 PC as % EQC	Stage 2 - Typical Values AC ($\mu g/m^3$)	PEC	PEC as % of EQC	Stage 3 - Monitored Data AC ($\mu g/m^3$)	PEC	PEC as % of EQC
Nitrogen oxides (NO_2)	Short term	200	139	70	77	216	108	69	208	104
	Long term	40	6.6	16	46	53	132	21	28	70
Particulates	Short term	50	17.5	35	44	62	124	37	55	110
Lead	Long term	0.5	0.013	2.6	0.05	0.063	12.6	0.035	0.048	9.6
Cadmium	Long term	0.005	0.0006	12	N/A	N/A	N/A	0.0008	0.0014	28

Metals

Lead

The national air quality information archive on the Internet provides annual average lead concentrations in air at a range of sites around the country. The nearest site is within 40km of our process. It shows an annual mean value of 0.035 mg m^{-3} and we use this value in Figure 4.16 to give a PEC value 0.048 mg m^{-3}. This is 10% of the EQC. However, lead in air is predominantly a local rather than regional issue and it would be prudent to check this assessment against monitored AC values for any national networks sites in localities with similar urban and industrial development and traffic densities to our site.

Other elements

There are currently only five multi-element monitoring stations in the UK that provide measurements of cadmium (and other metals). The data is reported in the Digest of Environmental Statistics, produced annually by the DETR. The nearest station that is most representative of our site is 120km away. In the absence of any better information we use this data in Figure 4.16. On this basis the PEC for cadmium is 28% of the EQC.

Comments on the AC estimates for air

- The use of typical values (Stage 2) provides a quick indication of which releases are likely to be a major problem. In this case it is clear at this stage that NO2 and PM10 are the pollutants of greatest concern.
- The long term ambient NO2 data provide a good example of the potential differences in Stage 2 and 3 assessments. The more accurate and more local monitored data (Stage 3) gave a significantly lower value for AC than the typical values. This gave a more reliable estimate of the PEC of around 70% of the EQC, compared with the Stage 2 estimate of 132% of the EQC.
- In this example we have used data to estimate AC from monitoring stations that are well outside the process footprint. If we were evaluating a proposed new process at a site that has releases of the same substances from other processes on the same site or within the process footprint, we would have to allow for the contribution those existing processes were making to the ambient levels.

Figure 4.17 gives a summary of the assessments we have made of the significant releases to air.

Figure 4.17 Comparison of PEC and EQC

Release situation	Substance	Temporal Basis	PC ($\mu g/m^3$)	AC ($\mu g/m^3$)	PEC ($\mu g/m^3$)	EQC ($\mu g/m^3$)	PEC/ EQC	Environmental Effect
A3	NO$_2$	Short term	139	69	208	200	1.04	High significance
A4	NO$_2$	Long term	6.6	21	28	40	0.70	High significance
A7	PM$_{10}$	Short term	17.5	37	55	50	1.1	High significance
A9	Cadmium	Long term	0.0006	0.0008	0.0014	0.005	0.28	Medium significance
A12	Lead	Long term	0.013	0.035	0.048	0.5	0.096	Marginal

The PEC/EQC ratios for both normal and peak releases of NO$_2$ and peak releases of PM$_{10}$ are greater than 0.4 and therefore of high significance. The normal release of cadmium has a PEC/EQC ratio in the range 0.1 to 0.4, which we classify as medium significance. The normal release of lead has a PEC/EQC ration below 0.1, but only just, and may be classified as marginal, but only if we are sure there are no other industrial sources of lead emissions within the *process footprint*.

The conclusions we draw from these assessments are:

- The normal releases of NO$_2$ and the metals cadmium and lead should be assessed more precisely using a more complex dispersion model, such as ADMS (see Appendix 2.4(k)) to check the validity of the results from the simple screening exercise we have carried out.
- The peak release rates of NO$_2$ and PM$_{10}$ are likely to cause occasional ground level concentrations above the NAQS targets for short term ground level concentrations of these pollutants. We should therefore look again at the process conditions that produce these peak emissions rates and consider how the process and its control systems could be modified to reduce these emissions.

To summarise, we have assessed the significance of the releases to air by comparing the RCs, PCs and PECs of the releases with the relevant EQC. The sequential screening process we have followed has enabled us to screen out the releases with very little environmental impact and to identify the releases that are most likely to have significant environmental impacts, requiring more detailed examination to determine their acceptability. The exercise is summarised in Figure 4.18, showing the practical implications that are likely to follow from these assessments.

Figure 4.18 Releases to air - their significance and the practical implications

Release situation	Substance	Temporal Basis	Environmental significance	Practical Implications		
				Analysis and Assessment Required	Control Required	Improvement Programme
A1	CO_2	Long term	Trivial	Estimate from fuel use	Normal combustion control	None
A2	CO	Short term	Trivial	Approximate, conservative methods and data acceptable	Process control monitoring and infrequent emission monitoring to check process performance	None
A3	NO_2	Short term	High significance	Accurate models and data required. Possible need for ambient quality monitoring	High level of process plant and release control with continuous monitoring of release rates	Urgent and substantial reduction of emissions
A4	NO_2	Long term	High significance	Accurate models and data required. Possible need for ambient quality monitoring	High level of process plant and release control with continuous monitoring of release rates	Probable need for planned reduction
A5	SO_2	Short term	Trivial	Approximate, conservative methods and data acceptable	Process control monitoring and regular emission monitoring to check process performance	None
A6	SO_2	Long term	Marginal, probably trivial	Approximate, conservative methods and data acceptable	Process control monitoring and infrequent emission monitoring to check process performance	None
A7	PM_{10}	Short term	High significance	Accurate models and data required. Possible need for ambient quality monitoring	High level of process plant and release control with continuous monitoring of release rates	Urgent and substantial reduction of emissions
A8	PM_{10}	Long term	Marginal, probably trivial	Approximate, conservative methods and data acceptable	Process control monitoring and infrequent emission monitoring to check process performance	None
A9	Cadmium	Long term	Medium significance	Accurate models and data required. Possible need for ambient quality monitoring	Process control monitoring and infrequent emission monitoring to check process performance	Examine scope for reducing emission rates in long term
A10	Chromium	Long term	Marginal, probably trivial	Approximate, conservative methods and data acceptable	Process control monitoring and infrequent monitoring to ensure long-term process performance	None
A12	Lead	Long term	Medium significance	Accurate models and data required. Possible need for ambient quality monitoring	Process control mopnitoring and frequent emission monitoring to check process performance	Examine scope for reducing emission rates in long term
A11 A13 A14	Copper Nickel Zinc	Long term	All trivial	Approximate, conservative methods and data acceptable.	Process control monitoring and regular emission monitoring to check peocess performance	

We have identified the releases to water in the emission inventory and the relevant release situations for each substance. Figure 4.4 gives the release concentrations (RC) of substances (all metals) in the effluent and the release rates. The release situations are summarised in Figure 4.8.

We now follow the same procedure as we did for releases to air, i.e. firstly we compare RC with EQC to screen out releases that are trivial because RC/EQC < 10; secondly we compare PC with EQC to screen out releases that are trivial because PC/EQC < 0.1; thirdly we compare PEC with EQC to assess level of significance of the remaining releases.

The results of this procedure are shown in Figure 4.19.

Figure 4.19 Comparisons of RC, PC and PEC with EQC for releases to water

Substance	EQC (µg/l)	RC (µg/l)	RC/ EQC	PC (µg/l)	PC/ EQC	AC (µg/l)	PEC (µg/l)	PEC/ EQC	PC/AC
Cadmium	2.5	130	52	0.5	0.20	0.05	0.55	0.22	10
Chromium	15	800	53	3.2	0.21	2.5	5.7	0.38	1.3
Iron	1000	100	0.1						
Lead	25	100	4	0.4	0.016	1.1			0.36
Zinc	40	2300	58	9.2	0.23	2.5	11.7	0.29	3.7

Stage 1: Comparing RC with EQC

Figure 4.19 shows that RC < EQC for iron and that RC < 10 x EQC for lead. The releases of these two metals may be regarded as trivial. However the value for lead is at the upper limit of this criterion. Lead is a widespread and toxic substance in water and it would therefore be prudent to continue the assessment of the lead release to the next stage.

Stage 2: Comparing PC with EQC

The discharge is to a tidal estuary. The effluent will disperse as a plume into the tidal flow. An appropriate formula for estimating dilution along the axis of an effluent plume is given in reference RS 8 (Appendix 2.4 (h)).

$$D = 30.7\, u_0\, /\, Q_v\, ,$$

where D is the dilution after 10 minutes of travel for an effluent discharging at a volume flow rate of 0.01 m^3 sec^{-1} (Q$_v$) on the bank of the estuary. We use the least favourable conditions for dilution by considering the discharge at slack water when the flow rate (u$_0$) past the outfall is only 0.08 m s^{-1}. This gives a value for D of 250 times dilution at the edge of the mixing zone. The distance to this point is the water flow rate (0.08 m s^{-1}) multiplied by the dilution time we have used (10 minutes or 600 seconds). This give a distance of 48 m which is a reasonable distance for the mixing zone in a large estuary at the time of least dilution.

We have calculated the PCs for cadmium, chromium, lead and zinc in this way and the results are shown in Figure 4.19. For lead the value of PC/EQC is less than 0.1 so we can consider it a marginal release. The values of PC/EQC for the other three metals are significant and we must take them to the next stage of assessment.

Stage 3: Comparing PEC with EQC

We will follow the procedure from Figure 3.10 to establish ambient quality data for the substances with releases that are potentially significant.

Stage 1: Is AC data required?

The results in Figure 4.19 show that we should establish AC data for cadmium, chromium and zinc.

Stage 2: Are released substances likely to be present in the receiving water?

All the metals we are considering are commonly present in many industrial and sewage treatment works effluents and they likely to be present in the estuary that receives the effluent from our process.

Stage 3: Is monitored data available for our watercourse?

Our process is located on an estuary where the width is approximately 1km. A monitoring station is located on the opposite side of the estuary about 1.9km upstream. This will provide ambient concentrations that are not likely to be influenced by our effluent. The monitoring site is operated by the Environment Agency for the purpose of classifying the general quality of the water in the estuary. It includes monthly sampling and analysis for the metals we are interested in. The data can be obtained from the Environment Agency as raw data or summary statistics, including the annual average ambient concentrations of metals.

Figure 4.19 shows the AC values obtained in this way, the resulting PEC values (PC + AC) and the ratios of PEC/EQC and PC/AC.

The values of PEC/EQC for the releases of cadmium, chromium, and zinc are in the range 0.1 - 0.4 which we rate as medium significance.

For all three metals it would now be advisable to assess their dispersion in the estuary more precisely, by using more sophisticated dispersion modelling techniques with more detailed information about the tidal flow patterns around the discharge point, to be sure that the discharges would not lead to any breach of an EQS.

Even if more detailed analysis showed that the releases would not lead to any breach of environmental quality standards in the estuary the Environment Agency would also require assurance that these discharges of heavy metals were the minimum that could be achieved by the use of BATNEEC. Negotiations under the OSPAR Commission are leading to international agreements to reduce discharges of harmful substances to the marine environment with the aim of reducing their concentrations to "near background" levels over the next 20 years. In this example you would have to show that the process incorporated all practicable techniques to minimise the amounts of heavy metals in the effluent.

The procedure we have used to assess the significance of releases of metals in the discharge to the estuary could also be used to assess the triviality or significance of other substances in the effluent, e.g. nitrates, ammonia, etc.

The emission inventory (Figure 4.4) also gives the pH and temperature of the effluent. We must check whether these properties of the effluent would be acceptable. For pH the statutory water quality objective for sea water is that pH should be between 6 and 8.5. Therefore an effluent pH of 8 is acceptable and there is no need for further assessment of this characteristic.

There are no statutory water quality objectives for temperature. In this case the discharge is a small volume and only 1°C higher in temperature than the receiving water. This characteristic in this situation can be considered as trivial *and there is no need for any further work to assess the potential effects of effluent temperature on the ecosystems in the estuary.*

Another consideration for discharges to water is the Environment Agency's "no significant deterioration"·policy when considering applications for consent for new discharges. This is described in Note 5 to Figure 3.10 in Chapter 3. In this example all the discharges of metals lead to a PC greater than 10% of the AC, so we would have to satisfy the Agency that there would be "insignificant environmental change" as a result of the discharges. This would involve the more complex dispersion modelling we have already mentioned for the discharges of cadmium, chromium and zinc that we have assessed as significant on the basis of PEC/EQC. We could also expect the Environment Agency to ask for a review of the process and its effluent treatment plant to see if it would be practicable to reduce the concentrations of metals in the effluent.

The releases to land result from deposition of airborne particulate matter containing metals. The release situations we will consider are shown in Figure 4.10.

Stage 1: Comparison of RC with EQC

The first stage of the procedure for air or water, namely comparing RC with EQC, is not relevant for assessing the significance of airborne deposition onto land. In this situation we are not looking at simple dilution of the release but at the accumulated contamination of surface soil by fall out and deposition from the dispersing airborne plume.

Stage 2: Comparing PC with EQC

We will use the tables in RS9 (Appendix 2.3j) to estimate the rate of deposition of metals from the two sources and then apply the formula given in section 2.3 to estimate the likely accumulated concentrations in surface soil over a 20 year lifetime of the plant.

We know from our estimates of atmospheric dispersion that maximum ground level concentrations will occur at some 800 m. from the 50 m. stack and some 200 m. from the extraction vent. Maximum deposition rates, for particles in the PM_{10} range, will occur at the same distances.

For the 50 m. stack with an effective discharge height of 80 m., the table in RS9 shows that 0.3% of material in the plume would be deposited between 500 and 1000 m. from the stack. For the 22 m. vent with an effective discharge height of 30 m., 0.5% of the release would be deposited between 200 and 500 m. and a further 1.2% between 500 and 1000 m. For an initial screening we will estimate the average combined deposition rate due to both sources over the area between 500 and 1000m. from the plant.

Figure 4.20 shows the results of these calculations.

Figure 4.20 Assessment of significance of airborne deposition to land

Release Situation	Substance	Deposition flux (mg/m²/day)	Accumulated load over 20 years (mg/kg) = PEC	EQC (mg/kb) (from Appendix 2.2d)	PEC/ EQC
L1	Cadmium	0.00041	0.038	3	0.013
L2	Chromium	0.00036	0.034	400	0.00085
L3	Copper	0.00057	0.053	135	0.00039
L4	Lead	0.0098	0.91	300	0.0030
L5	Nickel	0.0020	0.18	75	0.0024
L6	Zinc	0.0098	0.91	200	0.0046

Using the criteria of Figures 2.14 and 2.15, the PC/EQC ratios for deposition of chromium, copper are below 0.002 and may therefore be regarded as trivial in respect of this environmental impact. The ratios for cadmium, lead, nickel and zinc are all below 0.02 so these may be regarded as marginal. Bearing in mind the conservative assumptions we have made in compiling these estimates we may also rate these deposition rates as trivial and no further analysis is required.

If any of the estimated deposition rates had been > 2% of the EQC the next step would have been to consider the likely ambient concentrations of those metals in the area of the process footprint, using the typical data and references given in Note 4 to Figure 3.11. That would enable estimates to be made of PEC values for a further comparison with the EQC, using the criteria given in Figures 2.14 and 3.11.

It is very unlikely that airborne releases from a new process that meets the IPC requirements for BATNEEC and satisfies all environmental quality criteria for air, would lead to airborne deposition rates that would exceed environmental criteria for surface soil contamination.

Summary

In this worked example we have shown how the techniques for assessing the significance of release can be used as a screening procedure for identifying the relative environmental importance of the releases from a process. More detailed, and generally more costly, assessment can then be focussed on those areas where more precise assessment is required to ensure adequate protection of the environment.

The table in Figure 4.21 gives a pictorial summary of the assessments we have made for all the releases from the process. Such a summary, with the supporting tables we have developed as we worked through this example, would be useful in an IPC application. It demonstrates that there has been a systematic approach to assessing the environmental importance of the releases.

Figure 4.21 Summary of all releases

	Operational mode (air)	Trivial	Marginal	Medium significance	High significance
TO AIR					
CO	Peak	▓			
NO_2	Peak				▓
NO_2	Normal				▓
SO_2	Peak	▓			
SO_2	Normal		▓		
PM_{10}	Peak				▓
PM_{10}	Normal		▓		
Cadmium	Normal			▓	
Chromium	Normal		▓		
Copper	Normal				
Lead	Normal			▓	
Nickel	Normal	▓			
Zinc	Normal	▓			
TO WATER					
Cadmium				▓	
Chromium				▓	
Iron		▓			
Lead			▓		
Zinc				▓	
TO LAND					
Cadmium			▓		
Chromium		▓			
Copper		▓			
Lead			▓		
Nickel			▓		
Zinc			▓		

APPENDICES FOR CHAPTER 2

ENVIRONMENTAL QUALITY CRITERIA

Contents

Appendix 2.2 (a) Environmental quality criteria for substances in air

The lists of substances and environmental quality "standards" or "limits" in this Appendix are provided as examples of the information that can be used to determine appropriate EQCs for substances in air for the environmental analysis and assessment techniques that are recommended in this book.

EU Air Quality Standards

Sulphur Dioxide and Suspended Particulates: EU Directive 80/779/EEC

	Reference period	Limit Values (to be met by 1.4.83)
Sulphur Dioxide	One year (median daily values)	120 $\mu g/m^3$ if smoke less than 40 $\mu g/m^3$
		80 $\mu g/m^3$ if smoke more than 40 $\mu g/m^3$
	Winter (median of daily values)	180 $\mu g/m^3$ if smoke less than 60 $\mu g/m^3$
		130 $\mu g/m^3$ if smoke more than 60 $\mu g/m^3$
	Year, peak (98 percentile of daily values)	350 $\mu g/m^3$ if smoke less than 150 $\mu g/m^3$
		250 $\mu g/m^3$ if smoke more than 150 $\mu g/m^3$
Smoke	One year (median of daily value)	80 $\mu g/m^3$
	Winter (median of daily values)	130 $\mu g/m^3$
	Year, peak (98 percentile of daily values)	250 $\mu g/m^3$

		Guide values
Sulphur Dioxide	24-hour mean	100-150 $\mu g/m^3$
	One year mean	40-60 $\mu g/m^3$

Nitrogen Dioxide: EU Directive 85/203/EEC

	Reference period	Limit value (to be met by 1.7.87)
	One year (98 percentile of 1 hour means)	200 $\mu g/m^3$

		Guide values
	One year (50 percentile of 1 hour means)	50 $\mu g/m^3$
	One year (98 percentile of 1 hour means)	135 $\mu g/m^3$

Lead in the air: EU Directive 82/884/EEC

Limit Value (to be met by 9.12.87): 2 $\mu g/m^3$ annual mean

This table is reproduced from the NSCA 1998 Pollution Handbook, by kind permission of the National Society for Clean Air and Environmental Protection.

EU Proposed Limit values for Sulphur Dioxide, Nitrogen Dioxide, Particles and Lead

SO_2	350 $\mu g/m^3$, 1hr mean, (no more than 24 exceedances per year) to be achieved by 2005; 125 $\mu g/m^3$, 24hr mean; 20 $\mu g/m^3$, annual mean, for the protection of ecosystems.
NO_2	200 $\mu g/m^3$, 1hr mean, (no more than 8 exceedances per year) to be achieved by 2010; 40 $\mu g/m^3$, annual mean by 2010.
$NO + NO_2$	30 $\mu g/m^3$, annual mean, for the protection of vegetation.
Particles	50 $\mu g/m^3$, 24hr mean, (no more than 25 exceedances per year) to be achieved by 2005; 30 $\mu g/m^3$, annual mean, by 2005.
Lead	0.5 $\mu g/m^3$, annual mean by 2005.

This table is reproduced from the NSCA 1998 Pollution Handbook, by kind permission of the National Society for Clean Air and Environmental Protection.

National Air Quality Standards and Objectives

Pollutant	Standard Concentration	Measured as	Objective to be achieved by 2005
Benzene	5 ppb	Running annual mean	5 ppb
1-3-Butadiene	1 ppb	Running annual mean	1 ppb
Carbon monoxide	10 ppm	Running 8-hour mean	10 ppm
Lead	0.5 μg/m^3	Annual mean	0.5 μg/m^3
Nitrogen dioxide	150 ppb	1 hour mean	150 ppb, hourly mean*
	21 ppb	Annual mean	21 ppb, annual mean*
Ozone	50 ppb	Running 8-hour mean	50 ppb, measured as the 97th percentile*
Fine Particles (PM10)	50 μg/m^3	Running 24-hour mean	50 μg/m^3 measured as the 99th percentile*
Sulphur Dioxide	100 ppb	15 minute mean	100 ppb measured as the 99.9th percentile*

* provisional objectives – all to be reviewed in 1999; the percentiles mean: ozone target to be achieved on all but 10 days per year; particles target to be achieved on all but 4 days per year; sulphur dioxide standard to be achieved on all but 35 periods of 15 minutes, assuming complete data capture in a year.

This table is reproduced from the NSCA 1998 Pollution Handbook, by kind permission of the National Society for Clean Air and Environmental Protection.

WHO Air Quality Guidelines

Substances	Time-weighted average	Averaging time
Classical air pollutants		
Nitrogen dioxide	200 μg/m^3	1 hour
	40 μg/m^3	annual
Ozone	120 μg/m^3	8 hour
Sulphur dioxide	500 μg/m^3	10 minutes
	125 μg/m^3	24 hour
	50 μg/m^3	annual
Carbon monoxide	100 mg/m^3	15 minutes
	60 mg/m^3	30 minutes
	30 mg/m^3	1 hour
	10 mg/m^3	8 hours
Particulate matter	Exposure effect information to be provided giving guidance on major health impacts for short and long term exposures at various levels.	
Organic pollutants		
PAH (benzo-a-pyrene)	8.7 x 10^{-5} (ng/m^3)$^{-1}$	lifetime
Benzene	6 x 10^{-6} (μg/m^3)$^{-1}$	lifetime
Inorganic Pollutants		
Lead	0.5 μg/m^3	annual
Arsenic	1.5 x 10^{-3} (μg/m^3)$^{-1}$	lifetime
Cadmium	5 ng/m^3	annual
Mercury	1.0 μg/m^3	annual

This table is reproduced from the NSCA 1998 Pollution Handbook, by kind permission of the National Society for Clean Air and Environmental Protection.

These values were published by the World Health Organisation in 1987 as *Air Quality Guidelines for Europe*. They are generally accepted as levels not to be exceeded to maintain healthy air quality, but they are not mandatory. They are useful for IPC applicants in that they give EQC values for substances which are not yet covered by UK or EU standards.

Occupational Exposure Limits (OEL) 1997, published by the Health & Safety Executive (from HSE Books, PO Box 1999, Sudbury, Suffolk CO10 6FS, Tel: 01787 881165, Fax 01787 313995).

These are limits for the concentrations of substances, in the air in work places, that are considered adequate for protecting the health of people at work. OELs are normally quoted as 8 hr. time weighted average values. Some substances also have maximum allowable concentrations. Limit values are given for over 500 substances.

If there are no statutory or recommended EQC values for a substance the OEL may be used as a starting point for deriving an EQC value that would be adequate for assessing the significance of a release to air. Most people would accept that an EQC for public health protection should give a higher level of protection for public health, where exposure is involuntary, than for occupational health protection where exposure is voluntary and there is direct individual benefit from the activity. An additional safety factor of 10 would generally be advisable but consideration should always be given to the particular health effects caused by the substance to see if a different safety margin would be more appropriate.

As a general rule, use of an EQC derived from an OEL, should be limited to assessing whether a release is trivial or significant. If this screening assessment shows that the release is *significant*, you should seek specialist advice and/or consult the Environment Agency to determine a more reliable EQC value for the released substance based on its environmental fate and toxicological or eco-toxicological properties.

Appendix 2.2(b) Substances listed in UK or EC environmental protection legislation because of their potential to cause harmful effects in the environment.

There is no single comprehensive list of substances that are potentially harmful in the environment. In this Appendix we identify a selection of lists of substances that are specified in various UK and EC statutes for particular forms of control to protect public health and the environment.

Prescribed substances for Integrated Pollution Control

Releases into air

Oxides of sulphur and other sulphur compounds

Oxides of nitrogen and other nitrogen compounds

Oxides of carbon

Organic compounds and partial oxidation products

Metals, metalloids and their compounds

Asbestos (suspended particulate matter and fibres), glass fibres and mineral fibres

Halogens and their compounds

Phosphorus and its compounds

Particulate matter

Releases into water

Substance	Amount in excess of background quantity released in any 12 month period (Grammes)	
Mercury and its compounds	200	(expressed as metal)
Cadmium and its compounds	1000	(expressed as metal)
All isomers of hexachlorocyclohexane	20	
All isomers of DDT	5	
Pentachlorophenol and its compounds	350	(expressed as PCP)
Hexachlorobenzene	5	
Hexachlorobutadiene	20	
Aldrin	2	
Dieldrin	2	
Endrin	1	
Polychlorinated biphenyls	1	
Dichlorvos	0.2	
1,2-Dichloroethane	2000	
All isomers of trichlorobenzene	75	
Atrazine	350*	
Simazine	350*	
Tributyltin compounds	4	(expressed as TBT)
Triphenyltin compounds	4	(expressed as TPT)
Trifluralin	20	
Fenitorothion	2	
Azinphos-methyl	2	
Malathion	2	
Endosulfan	0.5	

* Where both Atrazine and Simazine are released, the figure in aggregate is 350 grammes.

Organic solvents	Oxidising agents
Azides	Polychlorinated dibenzofuran and any cogener thereof
Halogens and their covalent compounds	Polychlorinated dibenzo-p-dioxin and any cogener thereof
Metal carbonyls	Polyhalogenated biphenyls, terphenyls and napthalenes
Organo-metallic compounds	Phosphorus

Pesticides, that is to say, any chemical substance or preparation prepared or used for destroying any pest, including those used for protecting plants or wood or other plant products from harmful organisms; regulating the growth of plants; giving protection against harmful creatures; rendering such creatures harmless; controlling organisms with harmful or unwanted effects on water systems, buildings or other structures, or on manufactured products; or protecting animals against ectoparasites.

Alkali metals and their oxides and alkaline earth metals and their oxides.

These lists are reproduced from the NSCA 1998 Pollution Handbook, by kind permission of the National Society for Clean Air and Environmental Protection

The above list of prescribed substance in releases to water is also known as the *UK Red List*. These substances, together with carbon tetrachloride, are also prescribed substances under the trade Effluents (Prescribed Substances and Processes) Regulations, 1989, as amended.

Main Polluting Substances to be taken into account for IPPC

Taken from Annex II to EC Directive 96/61/EC on integrated pollution prevention and control

In releases to air:

1. Sulphur dioxide and other sulphur compounds
2. Oxides of nitrogen and other nitrogen compounds
3. Carbon monoxide
4. Volatile organic compounds
5. Metals and their compounds
6. Dust
7. Asbestos (suspended particulates, fibres)
8. Chlorine and its compounds
9. Fluorine and its compounds
10. Arsenic and its compounds
11. Cyanides
12. Substances and preparations which have been proved to possess carcinogenic or mutagenic properties or which may affect reproduction via the air
13. Polychlorinated dibenzodioxins and polychlorinated dibenzofurans

In releases to water:

1. Organo-halogen compounds and substances which may form such compounds in the aquatic environment.
2. Organo-phosphorous compounds
3. Organo-tin compounds
4. Substances and preparations which have been proved to possess carcinogenic or mutagenic properties or which may affect reproduction in or via the aquatic environment
5. Persistent hydrocarbons and persistent and bioaccumulable organic toxic substances
6. Cyanides
7. Metals and their compounds
8. Arsenic and its compounds
9. Biocides and plant health products
10. Materials in suspension
11. Substances which contribute to eutrophication (in particular, nitrates and phosphates)
12. Substances which have an unfavourable influence on the oxygen balance (and can be measured using parameters such as BOD, COD, etc.)

Appendix 2.2(c) Environmental quality criteria for substances in surface waters

The following summaries of current (August 1997) environmental quality standards applicable in UK waters, have been compiled by Zeneca's Brixham Environmental Laboratory.

Summary of current environmental quality standards for pesticides applicable in UK waters (Values in ug/l as Annual Averages, MAC values in brackets)

Substance	Statutory EQS		Advisory EQS	
	Freshwater	Seawater	Freshwater	Seawater
Abamectin			0.01 (0.03)	0.003 (0.01)
Aldrin	0.01	0.01		
Atrazine (+ Simazine)	2	2	(10)	(10)
Azamethiphos			0.02 (0.05)	0.02 (0.05)
Azinphos methyl	0.01	0.01	(0.04)	(0.04)
Bentazone	500	500	(5000)	(5000)
Bromoxynil			100 (1000)	100 (1000)
Bromoxynil octanoate			(1)	(1)
Carbendazim			0.1 (1)	0.1 (1)
Chlorfenvinphos			0.01 (0.1)	0.01 (0.1)
Chlorphenylid	0.05	0.05		
Chlorpropham			28 (40)	28 (40)
Chlorthalonil			0.1 (1)	0.1 (1)
Chlortoluron			2 (20)	2
Coumaphos			0.01 (0.1)	0.04 (0.4)
Cyfluthrin	0.001	0.001		
2,4-D (non-ester forms)	40	40	(200)	(200)
2,4-D (ester)	1	1	(10)	(10)
DDT	0.01	0.01		
Demetons (in total)			0.05 (0.5)	0.05 (0.5)
Demetons (UK Approved)	0.5	0.5	(5)	(5)
Diazinon			0.01 (0.1)	0.015 (0.15)
Dichlorvos	0.001	0.04 (0.6)		
Dieldrin	0.01	0.01		
Diflubenzuron			0.001 (0.015)	0.005 (0.1)
Dimethoate	1	1		
Diuron			2 (20)	2

Substance	Statutory EQS		Advisory EQS	
	Freshwater	Seawater	Freshwater	Seawater
Doramectin			0.001 (0.010)	0.001 (0.010)
Endosulfan	0.003	0.003	(0.3)	
Endrin	0.005	0.005		
Fenchlorphos			0.01 (0.1)	0.01 (0.1)
Fenitrothion	0.01	0.01	(0.25)	(0.25)
Flucofuron	1	1		
Hexachlorocyclohexane (Lindane)	0.1	0.02		
Ioxynil			10 (1000)	10 (1000)
Isodrin	0.005	0.005		
Isoproturon			2 (20)	2
Ivermectin			0.0001 (0.001)	0.001 (0.01)
Linuron	2	2	(20)	
Malachite Green Oxalate			0.5 (100)	0.5
Malathion	0.01	0.02	(0.5)	(0.5)
Maneb			3 (30)	3 (30)
Mancozeb			2 (20)	2 (20)
MCPA			25 (250)	25 (250)
Mecoprop	20	20	(200)	(200)
Methiocarb			0.01 (0.16)	0.01 (0.16)
Melvinphos	(0.02)			(1)
Omethoate	0.01			
Pendimethalin			1.5 (6)	1.5 (6)
Permethrin	0.01	0.01		
Pirimicarb			1 (5)	1 (5)
Pirimiphos-methyl			0.015 (0.05)	0.015 (0.15)
Prochloraz			4 (40)	4 (400
Propetamphos			0.01 (0.1)	0.01 (0.1)
Propyzamide			100 (1000)	100 (1000)
Simazine (+ Atrazine)	2	2	(10)	(10)
Sulcofuron	25	25		
Tecnazene			1 (100	1 (10)
Thiabendazole			5 (50)	5 (50)
Triallate			0.25 (5)	0.25 (5)
Triazophos	0.005	0.005	(0.05)	(0.05)
Trifluralin	0.1	0.1	(20)	(20)

Summary of current environmental quality standards
For organic compounds (excluding pesticides) applicable in UK waters
(Values in ug/l as Annual Averages, MAC values in brackets)

Substance	Statutory EQS		Advisory EQS	
	Freshwater	Seawater	Freshwater	Seawater
Benzene	30	30	(300)	
Biphenyl	25	25		
Carbon Tetrachloride	12	12		
Chlorobenzene			5	
Chloroform	12	12		
Chloromethylphenol	40	40	(200)	
Chlorotrotoluenes (in total)	10	10	(100)	
4 Chloro 3 nitrotoluene			10 (100)	
Chlorophenol (2)	50	50	(250)	
Chlorophenol (2, 3 or 4 in total)			50 (250)	
Dichlorobenzenes (in total)			20 (200)	
Dichloroethane (1,2)	10	10		
Dichlorophenol (2,4)	20	20	(140)	
Formaldehyde			5 (50)	
Hexachlorobenzene	0.03	0.03		
Hexachlorobutadiene	0.1	0.1		
Napthalene	10	5	(100)	(80)
Nonyl phenol			1 (2.5)	1 (2.5)
Octyl phenol			1 (2.5)	1 (2.5)
Pentachlorophenol	2	2		
Phenol			30 (300)	30 (300)
Phthalate - Butylbenzyl			20 (100)	20 (100)
Phthalate - Dibutyl (Total)			8 (40)	8 (40)
Phthalate - Diethyl			200 (1000)	200 (1000)
Phthalate - Dimethyl			800 (4000)	800 (4000)
Phthalate - Dioctyl (Total inc. DEHP)			20 (40)	20 (40)
Styrene			50 (500)	50 (500)
Tetrachloroethylene	10	10		
Tin (Organic - Tributyl tin oxide)	(0.02)	(0.002)		

Substance	Statutory EQS		Advisory EQS	
	Freshwater	Seawater	Freshwater	Seawater
Tin (Organic - Tricyclohexyl)	0.1			
Tin (Organic - Triphenyl)	(0.02)	(0.008)		
Tolulene	50	40	(500)	(400)
Tributyl Phosphate			50 (500)	50 (500)
Trichlorobenzene (sum of Isomers)	0.4	0.4		
Trichloroethane (1,1,1)	100	100	(1000)	(1000)
Trichloroethane (1,1,2)	400	300	(4000)	(3000)
Trichloroethylene	10	10		
Xylene	30	30	(300)	(300)

Summary of current environmental quality standards for inorganic compounds applicable in UK waters
(Values in ug/l as Annual Averages, MAC values in brackets)

Substance	Statutory EQS		Advisory EQS	
	Freshwater	Seawater	Freshwater	Seawater
Aluminium (Inorg Monomeric) pH<6.5			(10)	(10)
Aluminium (Inorg Monomeric) pH>6.5			15 (25)	15 (25)
Arsenic	50	25		
Boron	2000	7000		
Bromine (as Total Residual Oxidant)			2 (5)	(10)
Cadmium	5	2.5		
Chloride			250000	
Chlorine (as Total Residual Oxidant)			2 (5)	(10)
Chromium	5 - 250	15	2 - 20	5
Cobalt			3 (100)	3 (100)
Copper	1 - 28	5	0.5 - 12	5
EDTA			400 (4000)	400 (4000)
Fluoride (@ <50 mg/l CaCO3)			1000 (3000)	
Fluoride (@ >50 mg/l CaCO3)			5000 (15000)	5000 (15000)

Substance	Statutory EQS		Advisory EQS	
	Freshwater	Seawater	Freshwater	Seawater
Iron	1000	1000	300	300
Lead	4 - 250	25	4 - 20	10
Manganese			30 (300)	Insuff. data
Mercury	1	0.3		
Nickel	8 - 200	30	8 - 40	15
NTA			1000 (10000)	3000 (30000)
Oxygen			5000 - 9000	5000 - 9000
pH	6.0 - 9.0	6.0 - 8.5		
Silver			0.05 (0.1)	0.5 (1)
Sodium			170000	
Sulphate			400000	
Sulphide			0.25	10
Tin (Inorganic)			25	10
Vanadium	20 - 60	100		
Zinc	8 - 500	40	8 - 50	10

STATUTORY EQS

This is a statutory standard which applies to all waters throughout the UK

ADVISORY EQS

This has no statutory basis, but it has been derived for the DETR or the EA/SEPA using a standardised methodology. These values have been accepted by DETR/EA/SEPA, after peer review, as being the most appropriate standards. The EA and SEPA can be expected to use these values to derive individual emission limits. However, unlike the statutory EQSs, they do not have to be applied universally and site-specific circumstances can be taken into account.

Appendix 2.2(d) Environmental quality criteria for substances in soil

The following table and notes are taken from the Department of the Environment Code of Practice for Agriculture Use of Sewage Sludge.

Maximum permissible concentrations of potentially toxic elements in soil after application of sewage sludge and maximum annual rates of addition

PTE	Maximum permissible concentration of PTE in soil mg/kg dry solids)				Maxumum permissible average annual rate of PTE addition over a 10 year period (kg/ha)
	pH 5.0<5.5	pH 5.5<6.0	pH 6.0<7.0	pH >7.0	
Zinc	200	250	300	450	15
Copper	80	100	135	200	7.5
Nickel	50	65	75	110	3
	For pH 5.0 and above				
Cadmium	3				0.15
Lead	300				15
Mercury	1				0.1
Chromium	400				15
Molybdenum	4				0.2
Selenium	3				0.15
Arsenic	50				0.7
Fluoride	500				20

Notes to table:

1. The permitted concentrations of zinc, copper, cadmium and lead are provisional and will be reviewed when research into their effects on soil fertility and livestock is complete.
2. The annual rate of application of PTE to any site shall be determined by averaging over the 10 year period, ending with the year of calculation.
3. The increased permissible PTE concentrations in soils of pH greater than 7.0 apply only to soils containing more than 5% calcium carbonate.
4. The accepted safe level of molybdenum in agricultural soil is 4 mg/kg. However there are some areas in UK where, for geological reasons, the natural concentration of this element in soils exceeds this level. In such cases there may be no additional problems as a result of applying sludge, but this should not be done except in accordance with expert advice. This advice will take into account the molybdenum content of the sludge, existing soil molybdenum levels and the current arrangements to provide copper supplements to livestock.

Appendix 2.3 Dispersion Methods

Appendices 2.3 (a) to (j) provide summaries of the dispersion methods that are quoted in section 2.3 as quick methods that can be used for screening releases for their significance.

These summaries are not intended as work books for all the methods described. The aim of these Appendices is simply to give you sufficient information about the methods to help you decide which is the most appropriate for your particular situation.

The Table below gives the full titles of these reference sources.

Reference Summary (RS)	Title
RS1	*Technical Guidance Note (Dispersion) D1 - Guidelines on Discharge Stack Heights for Polluting Emissions,* published by HMSO for Her Majesty's Inspectorate of Pollutants 1993
RS2	Turner B., (1991) *Workbook of Atmospheric Dispersion Estimates: An Introduction to Dispersion Modelling,* 2nd edition, published by Lewis Publishers
RS3	Clarke R. H., (1979), *A Model for Short and Medium Range Dispersion of Radionuclides Released to the Atmosphere, (R91)* The first report of a working group on atmospheric dispersion for the National Radiological Protection Board
RS4	Valentin F. H., North AA, *Odour Control - A Concise Guide,* (1980), published by Warren Spring Laboratory on behalf of the DoE
RS5	Woodfield M. and Hall D., (1994), *Odour Measurement and Control - An Update,* Warren Spring Laboratory LR 965
RS6	Price D. R. H and Pearson M. J., (1979), T*he Derivation of Quality Conditions for Effluents Discharged to Freshwaters,* Published in Water Pollution Control 1979 for the Anglian Water Authority
RS7	Lewis R., (1997), *Dispersion in Estuaries and Coastal Waters,* John Wiley and Sons, Chichester
RS8	National Rivers Authority (1994), *Discharge Consent and Compliance - The NRA's Approach to Control of Discharge to Water*
RS9	Jones J. A., (1981) *A Procedure to include Deposition in the Model for Short and Medium Range Atmospheric Dispersion of Radionuclides (Report NPPB-R122.)* Report by the working group on atmospheric dispersion (now the Atmospheric Dispersion Modelling Liaison Committee) for the National Radiological Protection Board.

Appendix 2.3(a) Reference Summary RS1 - Technical Guidance Note (Dispersion (D1) - Guidelines on Discharge Stack Heights for Polluting Emissions

Purpose and Scope

To provide a method for ensuring that stack heights provide suitable dispersion of airborne emissions to protect public health and the environment. It can also be used to assess the dispersion from existing stacks. It is intended for use by both industry and regulators. The method is based on results obtained from the R-91 model (Appendix 2.3(c)) for different stack heights and a range of efflux and meteorological conditions. It is specifically tailored for estimating dispersion of airborne pollutants from combustion processes but it can be used for other airborne releases from manufacturing processes provided that the calculated values are within the applicable range of the method. The guidance note includes worked examples and it is easy to use.

Calculation Method

The calculation uses simple equations and nomograms to give approximate estimates of stack heights (or dilution rates) for a wide range of release rates and efflux conditions. An estimate should typically take between 1 and 2 hours. The calculation method is in three stages. The sequence for determining the minimum stack height for a new process is:

Stage 1 - Calculating the Pollution Index (Pi).

Pi is the average dilution rate in air (m^3/s) needed to reduce the concentration of the released substance to a specified maximum ground level concentration - usually the EQC as a 1 hour mean value.

- Identify released substances and release rates
- Determine the appropriate EQC
- Correct for any ambient concentrations of the same substances
- Calculate the pollution index, Pi (formula below) for each released substance
- Identify the released substance with highest value of Pi.

Stage 2 - Calculating the Discharge Stack Height

- Calculate plume rise due to heat release (Q) of the emission (formula below)
- Calculate plume rise due to emission exit velocity (formula below)
- Select the higher of the two plume rises as the determining factor
- Calculate required stack height, based on the substance with the highest Pi value, correcting for the presence of nearby tall structures if necessary

The nomogram in Figure A1 (taken from Figure 2 of the guidance note) can be used to estimate the required stack height for the Pi and Q you have calculated.

Stage 3 - Other Considerations, Cross-Checks and Adjustments

- Minimum discharge velocity and other flue exit conditions (*minimum discharge velocity must be 15 m.s⁻¹*)
- Overriding minimum requirements for discharge stack heights (*stack must be minimum of 3m above roof areas, gantries etc*)
- Discharge stack heights for plant with a wide operational range (*check chimney height estimate for high and low discharge rates*)
- Multiple sources, nearby sources and combining emissions (*if stacks are within distance of 3 stack diameters of each other, treat them as a single stack*)
- Difficult siting (*needs to be considered if tall buildings are nearby*)
- Highly abated emissions (*Consider likely release rates during malfunction of abatement equipment, provision of emergency stacks, visibility of plumes, etc.*)

Formulae

Pollution Index $P_i = \dfrac{D}{(G_d - B_c)} \times 1000$

Where D is the discharge rate of the pollutant (g/s), G_d is the guideline concentration of the discharged pollutant (mg/m³) and B_c is the background concentration of the discharged pollutant for a particular district/area (mg/m³).

The heat release value, Q in Figure 2 of the Guidance Note (Figure A1), is given by:

$$Q = \dfrac{V\left(1 - \dfrac{283}{T_d}\right)}{2.9}$$, in MW, where V is the total volume rate of discharge of gases (m³/ sec) and T_d is the

temperature of the discharging gases (°K).

Plume rise due to exit velocity is calculated by the formulae:

Momentum, $M = \dfrac{283}{T_d} \cdot V \cdot w$, where w is the discharge velocity (m/sec).

Momentum plume rise, $U_m = 0.82M^{0.32}$

Advantages

- Method is recognised by the Environment Agency and Local Authorities
- Method has an explanatory background document
- The calculation method is simple
- Method can be used for estimating required chimney heights for proposed releases, or maximum ground level concentrations of releases from existing chimneys
- Method can be adapted for odours

Limitations

- Only short term impacts are considered.
- Limited to a range of 100 stack heights from source
- Restricted to steady continuous discharges, ejected vertically
- Not applicable for modelling short duration discharges, such as relief valves or accidental discharges
- Not generally applicable where slopes > 1:10
- Restricted to stack heights of 200m, and in range of 100 - 200 m stack heights derived are only approximate
- Method should only be used to give a first indication of stack height. In most situations more detailed modelling should be used for determining final stack height.
- Method is based on worst case meteorological conditions, but excludes strong winds in excess of 20 ms-1
- Does not include recent developments in modelling or allow for different averaging times that are specified in current air quality standards.

Figure A1 Estimation of Uncorrected Discharge Height from Pi and heat released (Q) at stack exit

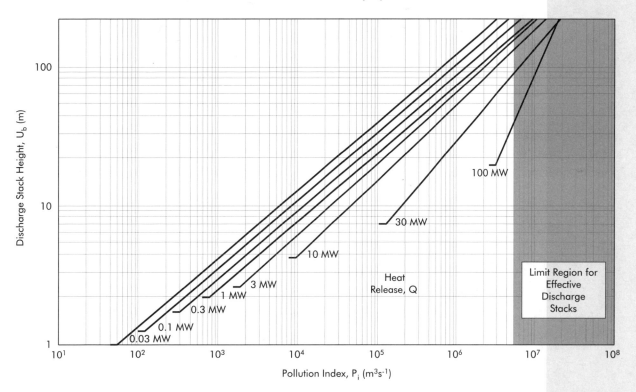

This nomogram, taken from Figure 2 of the Technical Guidance Note D1, shows the uncorrected discharge stack height plotted as a function of the Pollution Index and the heat release. It gives a minimum stack height assuming no complex effects from buildings or topography. The shaded area shows the values of the Pollution Index of around 10^7 and beyond.

Related Information

D1 has a background document - *Background to the New HMIP Guidelines on Determining Discharge Stack Heights for Polluting Emissions*, Hall D.J., Kukadia V (1993), Warren Spring Laboratory Report No. LR 929.

Clean Air and Environmental Protection, Volume 24 Number 2 Summer 1994, '*Approaches to the Calculation of Stack Heights for Odour Control*', Hall D.J., Kukadia V. pages 74-92

Valentin F.H. and North A.A. (1980) *Odour Control - A Concise Guide*, published by Warren Spring Laboratory on behalf of the DoE, gives further details on chimney height assessment for odour emissions.

The United Kingdom National Air Quality Strategy document, published by DoE (now DETR) gives Air Quality Standards (AQSs).

Pasquill, F. and Smith, F.B., (1983) *Atmospheric Diffusion*. Ellis Horwood Ltd, Chichester.

Appendix 2.3 (b) Reference Summary RS2 - Workbook of Atmospheric Dispersion Estimates: An Introduction to Dispersion Modelling

Purpose and Scope

The workbook provides an introduction to dispersion calculations and dispersion modelling for readers new to this subject. It also provides a ready reference to dispersion equations and example calculations for air quality professionals already familiar with dispersion.

Contents

- Dispersion processes
- Rates of dispersion
- Effect of buoyancy at emission point
- Special topics - fluctuations; dosage from a short period release; estimation of seasonal or annual average concentration; contribution from multiple sources; rural and urban dispersion parameters; topography; area and line sources.

Features

Section 2.10 of the book provides a nomogram (reproduced as Figure A2 below) showing peak ground level concentration plotted against distance from the source for different stack heights and different atmospheric stability categories (as Pasquill categories A to F). The ground level concentrations (c) are normalised for wind speed u and the mass rate of release Q of a substance.

Section 3.3.1 of the book discusses effective height estimates. The effective height (H) of a release is the sum of the actual height of release (h) and the plume rise (Dh) due to the thermal buoyancy and the vertical momentum of the emissions. The magnitude of Dh is calculated for both momentum and buoyant rise, and the largest value is assumed to be the dominant mechanism.

Example

Consider a buoyant gas which is released from a source with an effective height of 15 m at a mass release rate of 10 g s^{-1}. The mean wind speed is 3 m s^{-1} and the stability of the atmosphere is category C. Estimate the maximum ground level concentration and the distance at which this will occur downwind from the release point.

Using Figure A2, the dimensionless number $(\chi u/Q)_{max}$ is about 6.0×10^{-4} m^{-2} for a release at 15 m under category C conditions. It follows that $\chi = 6.0 \times 10^{-4} \times 10/3.0$ g m$^{-3} = 2.0 \times 10^{-3}$ g m^{-3}. This is equivalent to a concentration of 2.0×10^{3} µg m^{-3}. Figure A2 also indicates that this maximum value would occur at a downwind distance of approximately 0.13 km (i.e. 130 m).

Section 2.1.1 of the book discusses the accuracy of the dispersion estimates. Estimated errors associated with source strength, wind speed and height of release are 10-25 % for each parameter; errors associated with the selection of a stability class are perhaps 30 %; errors in the lateral and vertical spreading rates may be as much as 100 %, depending on the stability and distance of travel. Even where the magnitude of the maximum downwind concentration has been estimated quite well, the effect of changes in wind speed and direction with height may mean that the location of the peak concentration is incorrect.

General Comments

Turner explains that a simple Gaussian model, which is the basis for Figure.A2, is not suitable for predicting concentrations under convective conditions or for ground level releases. It can be seen from the figure that predicted concentrations are particularly sensitive to the effective height of release - hence, the allowance for buoyant rise is a critical aspect of any concentration estimate. In broad terms, Figure A2 can be used to derive simple screening formulae for estimating the maximum downwind concentration for a given stack height with an *error* of perhaps a factor of 2, i.e. a value of 30µg/m^{-3} determined by this method should be interpreted as being within the range 15 to 60 µg/m^{-3}.

Figure A2 Nomogram showing peak Ground Level Concentrations and Distance for different stack heights and Pasquill stability categories

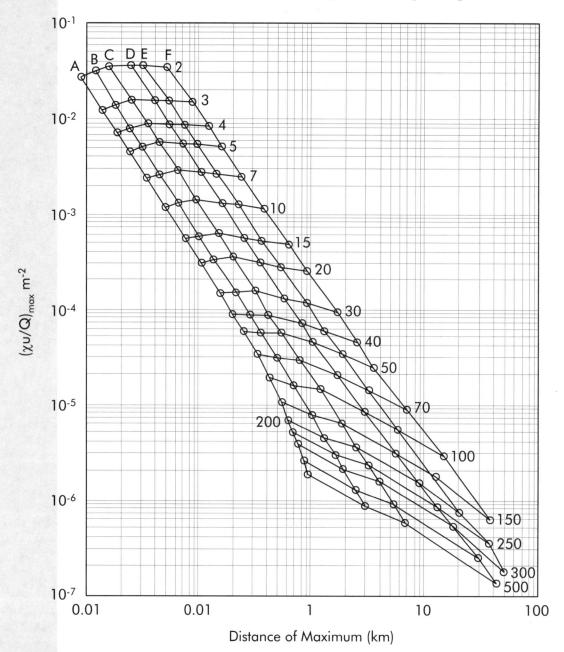

Appendix 2.3 (c) Reference Summary RS3 - A Model for Short and Medium Range Dispersion of Radionuclides Released to the Atmosphere

Purpose and Scope

This report is the first of a series setting out the recommendations of a working group on atmospheric dispersion of emissions containing radio-active substances. It recommends a basic model for predicting the dispersion of pollutants released to air over distances of up to a few tens of kilometres. Although the title and the text of the report refer to the dispersion of radioactive substances, the model is valid for other pollutants that move with air currents, i.e. gases (other than dense gases in very high concentrations) and fine particulates.

Contents

The main contents of the report are:
- the gaussian plume diffusion model
- choice of meteorological dispersion category
- choice of dispersion parameters
- accuracy of the predictions of the suggested model
- conditions for applicability of the proposed scheme
- representative results for dispersion from single sources

Features

The basic equations of the recommended gaussian plume diffusion model are given in the report. The equations relate the concentration of the released substance in the air in terms of the release rate of the substance, the height of the release, and a number of parameters which depend on the weather conditions. These weather conditions are described in terms of the Pasquill categories used by the Meteorological Office. The model can be used, for example, to calculate the maximum concentration that might result from a short release in "worst case" weather conditions, or the average annual concentration from a continuous release. The report gives values for the parameters used in the model equations. It also includes graphs giving the concentration at ground level for a unit release in each category of weather conditions, for a number of different release heights, and for both short and continuous releases.

As examples, Figures A3 and A4 reproduce figures 16 and 36 from the report. They show the relationship of ground level concentration with distance from the source for a range of release heights under particular weather conditions and release conditions. Figure A3 gives the model results for the short term ground level concentration directly downwind of a short term release under Pasquill category D weather conditions. Figure A4 gives the annual average concentration pattern around a release point for a continuous release under a typical mix of UK weather conditions.

Other graphs and diagrams can be used to take account of differing weather conditions and different durations of release. Figure A5, taken from Figure 11 of the report, shows the annual average distribution of Pasquill stability categories across the UK. Figure A6, taken from Figure 23 of the report, shows the relationship of ground level concentrations with release duration under Pasquill category D conditions.

These series of graphs provide ready reference nomograms for looking up the concentration at ground level for the release of unit amount of a substance as a function of distance from the release, for release heights from zero to 200 metres and for each of seven types of weather condition.

For example, using Figure A3 for a 30 minute release of, say, 10 grams of a substance occurring at a height of 30 metres in category D weather conditions, we can predict that the time integrated concentration of the substance at ground level at a downwind distance of 1 km will be 1.3×10^{-5} multiplied by 10 gram-seconds per cubic metre (or 1.3×10^{-4} gs/m^3). Anyone standing in the path of the pollutant plume as it passed would then have inhaled about 0.03 micrograms of the pollutant in the 30 minute period, assuming a normal breathing rate of 20 cubic metres per day.

A second set of graphs gives modifying factors to account for releases lasting up to 24 hours. For example, Figure A6 shows how the results shown in Figure A3 would be modified for releases lasting between 1 and 24 hours. If the 10 grams of pollutant were released over 6 hours rather than 30 minutes, the time integrated concentration at ground level at 1 km would be 0.45 (taken from Figure A6) times 1.3×10^{-4} gs/m^3 (or 5.9×10^{-5} gs/m^3).

Further sets of graphs give the ground level concentration resulting from the continuous release of unit amount of a substance in each type of weather condition. The graphs can be used selectively to allow ground level concentrations to be estimated according to the amount of weather information available. For example, Figure A4 shows a graph which can be used if there is little specific weather information available. It applies to a mixture of weather conditions in which category D conditions occur about 60% of the time, and assumes that the wind is equally likely to be in any direction. Figure A5 shows how the types of weather conditions vary around the UK. Figure A4 would apply to locations around the 60 contour in Figure A5. For an annual release of, say, 10 kilograms of pollutant released at a height of 30 metres, Figure A4 predicts that the time integrated concentration of the pollutant at ground level at a distance of 1 km would be 3.6×10^{-7} multiplied by 10,000 gs/m^3 (or 3.6×10^{-3} gs/m^3). This corresponds to an annual average concentration of 3.6×10^{-3} divided by 3.15×10^7 (the number of seconds in a year) grams per cubic metre (or about 0.11 nanograms per cubic metre).

Advantages

The look-up graphs provide a simple means for estimating concentrations of substances in air resulting from point-source releases in a variety of circumstances without the need for more complex computer programmes.

Limitations

Predictions of the model apply for distances of up to a few tens of kilometres from the release and to isolated releases (i.e. away from any buildings or other tall structures). They are thought to be accurate to within a factor of three for short duration releases and to within +/- 50% for annual average concentrations. The model used in this report does not take account of deposition from the air on to the ground.

Related Information

Later reports in the series show how the basic model can be modified to take account of buildings and wet and dry deposition processes. The second report - *A procedure to include deposition in the model for short and medium range atmospheric dispersion of radionuclides*, NRPB-R122 and the fifth report - *Models to allow for the effects of coastal sites, plume rise and buildings on dispersion of radionuclides and guidance on the value of deposition velocity and washout coefficients, NRPB-R157.*

Figure A3 Ground level concentrations as a function of release height for a short duration (30 minutes) unit release in Pasquill Category D conditions

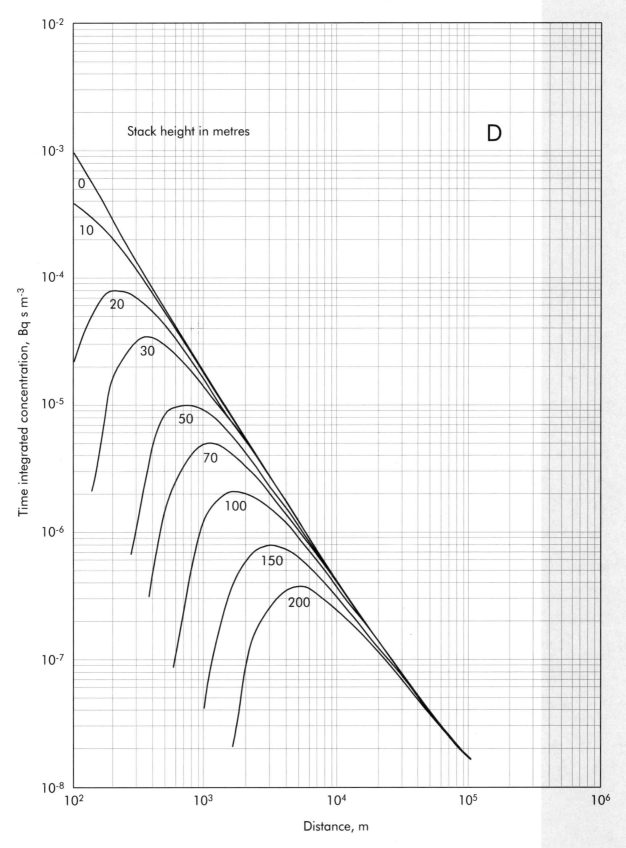

Stack height in metres

0
10
20
30
50
70
100
150
200

D

Time integrated concentration, Bq s m^{-3}

Distance, m

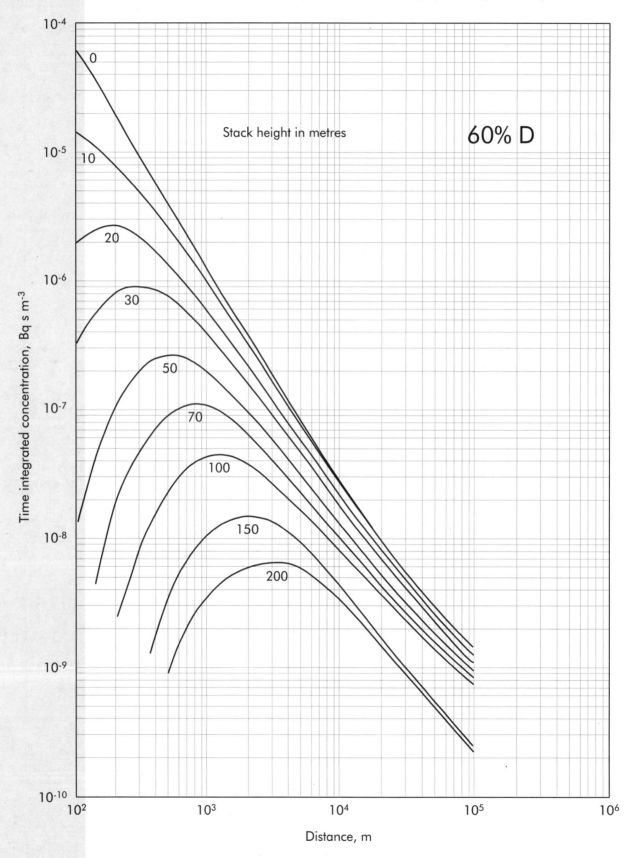

Figure A4   Ground level concentrations as a function of distance and effective stack height for unit rate of continuous release. A uniform wind rose is assumed and the frequency distribution of Pasquill categories corresponds to the 60% D contour of the UK Pasquill stability map (see Figure A5)

Figure A5 Frequency of occurrence of the Pasquill stability categories within the UK

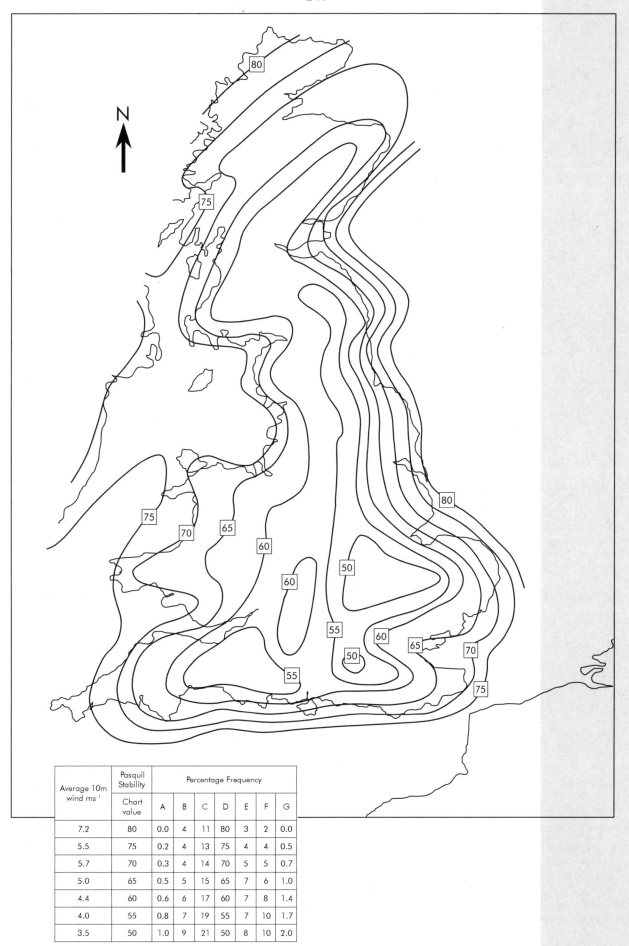

Average 10m wind ms⁻¹	Pasquil Stability	Percentage Frequency						
	Chart value	A	B	C	D	E	F	G
7.2	80	0.0	4	11	80	3	2	0.0
5.5	75	0.2	4	13	75	4	4	0.5
5.7	70	0.3	4	14	70	5	5	0.7
5.0	65	0.5	5	15	65	7	6	1.0
4.4	60	0.6	6	17	60	7	8	1.4
4.0	55	0.8	7	19	55	7	10	1.7
3.5	50	1.0	9	21	50	8	10	2.0

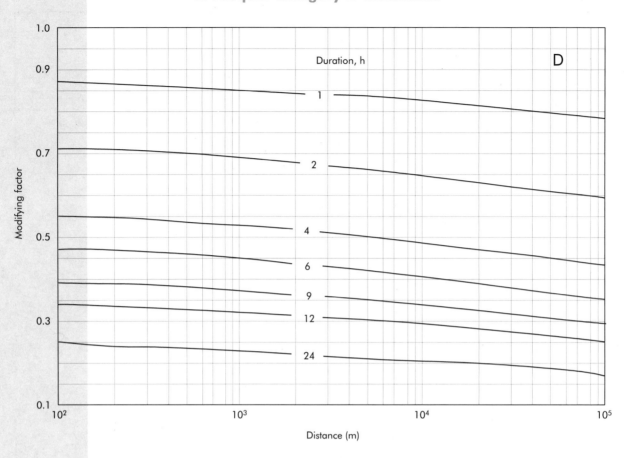

Figure A6 Ground level concentrations as a function of release duration in Pasquill Category D conditions

Appendix 2.3(d) Reference Summary RS4 - Odour control - A Concise Guide

Purpose and Scope

The book is based on the results of the 3 years' research programme into the measurement and control of odours carried out, largely by Warren Spring Laboratory, from 1975 - 1978. It's aim was to provide a guide for engineers, scientists and regulators who were concerned with the assessment and abatement of odour nuisances.

Main Contents

The areas covered are:
(a) Assessment of odours
(b) Human sense of smell and response to odours
(c) Legal position on odour nuisance
(d) Measurement of odours
(e) Odour control techniques: -   Incineration
                                 -    Oxidation
                                 -    Absorption
                                 -    Carbon adsorption
                                 -    Dispersion

Features

The guide uses the concepts of *odour units* and *odour dilution factors* to characterise odorous emissions. This approach is particularly useful for assessing odorous emissions that cannot be easily be characterised in terms of concentrations of specific compounds, such as the emissions from some animal product processes. The method allows "odour" to be treated the same way as a released "substance" for estimating dispersion and dilution in the atmosphere, using the gaussian plume model described in RS3 - see Appendix 2.3(c).

The odour dilution factor (D), required to reduce the concentration of an odorous emission to a level that is unlikely to cause a nuisance is given by: $D = \dfrac{\chi}{\chi_o}$,

where χ is the concentration of odorous substances at the chimney exit
        χ_o is the 50% odour detection threshold

Figure A7, taken from Table 3-1 of the guide, gives some typical odour emission figures (before abatement). It gives dilution factors, flowrates, odour emissions and typical abatement equipment for a number of different industries. (Some of this information may now be out of date.)

Advantages

- The main principles are still valid.
- It provides useful guidance for those who need to consider the assessment and abatement of odorous releases from processes.
- It gives rule of thumb guidance on recommended chimney heights for adequate dispersion of odours, based on the gaussian plume model.
- It discusses the relationships between odour emission rates and complaints, and between peak to mean concentrations of odours.

Limitations

Some of the information, particularly on abatement technology, is somewhat out of date.

Figure A7 Some Typical Odour Emission Figures (Before Abatement) and Dilution Factors

Industry		Dilution Factor	Flowrate (m³ s⁻¹)	Odour Emission (m³ s⁻¹)	Typical Abatement Equipment
Rendering					
100 t/wk	Ventilation	20,000	8.5		
	Process	42,000	0.75	Total 202,000	
200 t/wk	Ventilation	333,000	1.2		
	Process	217,000	0.35	Total 476,000	Ventilation:
350 t/wk	Ventilation	6,000	13.5		Absorbers
	Process	1,350,000	0.5	Total 756,000	
Approx. 600 t/wk	Ventilation	28,000	10.5		Process:
	Process	420,000	0.55	Total 525,000	Incineration
Approx 1500 t/wk	Ventilation	42,000	20		
	Process	340,000	0.45	Total 993,000	
Feather Hydrolosis					
			0.018	72,000	
			0.21	105,000	Absorbers
			0.08	320,000	
Maggot Farm					
2.5 to 3 x 10³ gal/wk (October)		5,000	6	30,000	Absorbers
Farming					
Pig pens		400 to 600	-	-	
Chicken House (15,000 birds)		600	4.2	2,520	None
Fishmeal					
White fish		150,000	7.9	1,185,000	Boiler
80% oily fish		400,000	7.9	3,160,000	Incinerators
Poultry Manure Drying					
8 t/h		200,000	6	1,200,000	
1 t/h		43,000	1.5	65,400	Incinerators
Less than 1 t/h		22,000	0.5	11,000	
Swill Boiling					
2.5 ton pressure cooker		17,000	0.95	16,200	Absorbers
Blood Drying					
500 gal batch		50,000	0.25	12,500	Incineration
Pharmaceuticals					
Sterilisation for fermenter		715,000	0.75	536,000	None/Absorbers
Potato Crisps					
30,000 t/yr		250,000	-	435,000	
100,000 t/yr		30,000	14.5	660,000	None/Absorbers
		275,00	2.4		
Printing					
Web-offset		40,000	1.5	60,000	
Low Pollution inks		2,000	2.0	4,000	Incineration
Textile Stentering					
Nylon		18,000	2.0	36,000	None/Catalytic
Polyester cotton		1,200	0.6	720	Incineration

Related Information

The principle UK legislation dealing with nuisance from odorous emissions is the Public Health Acts 1936 and 1969. The main statutory nuisance provisions are in Parts III of these Acts with other relevant provisions in Parts II and XI.

Odours. Report of the Working Party on the Suppression of Odours from offensive and selected other trades, Part 2. Stevenage: Warren Spring Laboratory, 1975.

Kinkley, M.L., and Deveril, R.B., (1970) *Capital and Operating Costs of Selected Air Pollution Control Systems*, US Environmental Protection Agency.

Industrial Ventilation – A Manual of Recommended Practice, (1970) American Conference of Government Industrial Hygienists.

Ames J. (1978), *Systems Study of Odorous Industrial Processes*. Stevenage: Warren Spring Laboratory, LR 287.

Appendix 2.3(e) Reference Summary RS5 - Odour measurement and control - An update

Purpose and Scope

As the title indicates, this is an update of the 1980 book (RS4, Appendix 2.3(d)) with new sections on Biotechnological Odour Control and Odour Threshold data. Odour dispersion and the determination of stack heights are based on the guidance given in the HMIP Technical Guidance Note D1, Guidelines on Discharge Stack Heights for Polluting Emissions (Appendix 2.3(a)). It was compiled to provide guidance for managers and regulators of Part B processes.

Contents

Apart from the update on dispersion and the additional information on biotreatment systems, it provides little more than the 1980 book which has more comprehensive coverage of the subject.

Features

It provides a useful method for determining stack heights for odorous emissions, as follows:

Odorous discharge rate (E) is defined as: $\quad E = \dfrac{D}{T} \; x \; 1000,$

where D is the discharge rate of the total emission in $g.sec^{-1}$
T is the odour threshold of the emission in $mg.m^{-3}$

Alternatively if the threshold rate is given in dilutions then: $\quad E = V \; x \; DTT$

where V is the volume discharge rate in $m^3.s^{-1}$
DTT is the number of dilutions to odour threshold in odour units.

Once the value of the odorous discharge rate (E) is calculated, this is multiplied by a factor of 10 to give the value for the Pollution Index (Pi). Guidance Note D1 (Appendix 2.3(a)) can then be used to determine a stack height, in the same way as for any other released substance. Equally, this method can be used, in reverse as it were, to estimate the ground level concentration, in relation to odour threshold, of an odorous emission from an existing stack to assess the likelihood of causing offence.

Advantages

It provides useful guidance for:

- determining chimney heights to achieve adequate dispersion of odours
- relating modelled 3 minute average concentrations to odour detection timescales.
- the relationship between odour emission rates and complaints by the public
- odour threshold data that can be used for chimney height assessments and complaint investigations.

Limitations

- There is very little guidance given on the issue of significance and triviality
- It adds little new information to the 1980 publication.

Related Information

AFNOR X 43 - 101E, *Atmospheric Pollution: Method of measurement of the odour of a gaseous effluent*, November 1991.

Hall, D.J., Kukadia, V., 1993, *Approaches to the Calculation of Discharge Stack Heights for Odour Control.* Warren Spring Laboratory Report LR 994.

Cheremisinoff P.N. and Young R.A., (1977), *Air Pollution Control and Design Handbook*, Marcel Dekker.

Appendix 2.3(f) Reference Summary RS6 - The Derivation of Quality Conditions for Effluents Discharged to Freshwaters

Purpose and Scope

This document provides a method for deriving effluent quality limits for discharges that are upstream from the freshwater limit of a watercourse.

Contents

The document reviews the historic approach to the determination of discharge consents. It contains a calculation method based on a steady state mass balance of discharges into a watercourse.

Features

The freshwater limit is defined as the point where the salinity is 200 mg/l.

The calculation method for determining permitted discharges, based on downstream water quality standards, assumes that there is immediate and ideal mixing at the point of discharge. This means that a discharge is assumed to mix uniformly over the whole cross section of the watercourse as soon as it enters the water and that there is no loss of material, e.g. through decomposition or deposition.

The user has to assign one of three river categories to the receiving water course, based on river flow conditions. He must also assign classifications of uses for various stretches of the water course as illustrated in Figure A8.

The method covers five main steps:

- Construction of a classification system of river uses
- Formulation of water quality criteria for these various uses
- Development of river quality specifications based upon above
- Selection of flow and quality conditions to be adopted for design purposes in the calculation of discharge quality conditions.
- Calculation of required quality / consent conditions by mass balance

The mass balance method for determining the maximum permitted concentration of a controlled substance in a proposed discharge is illustrated in Figure A9.

Advantages

- The method is simple because it is based on steady state model.
- It provides a concise historic background to the development of procedures for determining consents to discharge.

Limitations

- The historic background is now out of date.
- The method assumes that the user has access to information on other discharge conditions upstream and downstream.
- The user must assess the category of the river into which the effluent will be discharged.
- The method does not take account of more recent developments in river water quality management, e.g. Statutory Water Quality Objectives.
- The river classification method, based on river velocity, may only be applicable to the Anglian region.

Related Information

Recommendations for Statutory Water Quality Objectives (SWQOs) published by the Environment Agency.

Rutherford, J.C. (1994) *River Mixing*, John Wiley and Sons Ltd., Chichester.

Figure A8 Typical classification of River Use

In this illustration six different stretches of river are classified according to their uses.(These classifications would now be incorporated in the Environment Agency's Local Environment Agency Plan (LEAP) which would set out the measures planned to manage each stretch of the river.)

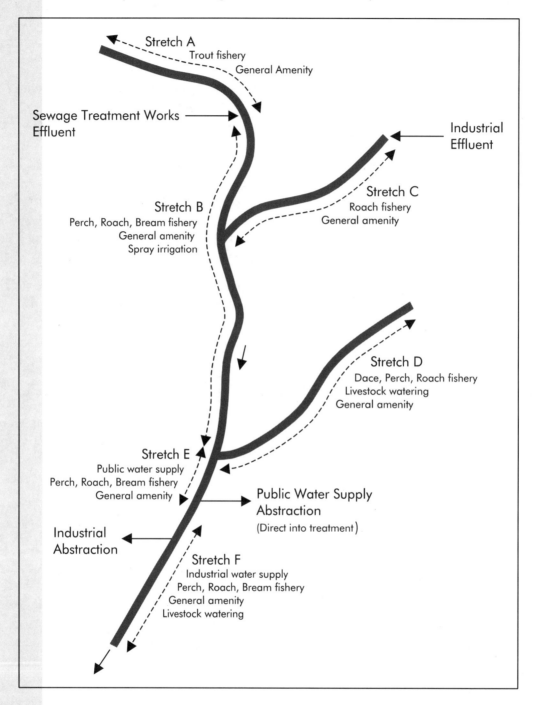

Stretch A
Trout fishery
General Amenity

Sewage Treatment Works
Effluent

Industrial
Effluent

Stretch C
Roach fishery
General amenity

Stretch B
Perch, Roach, Bream fishery
General amenity
Spray irrigation

Stretch D
Dace, Perch, Roach fishery
Livestock watering
General amenity

Stretch E
Public water supply
Perch, Roach, Bream fishery
General amenity

Public Water Supply
Abstraction

(Direct into treatment)

Industrial
Abstraction

Stretch F
Industrial water supply
Perch, Roach, Bream fishery
General amenity
Livestock watering

Figure A9 Calculation of consent conditions by mass balance

Upstream	Proposed Discharge	Downstream

<u>Natural flow conditions*</u>
   Flow: FRU (m³/hr)
   Concentration of controlled substances: CRU (mg/m³)
 	
<u>Effluent (entering river upstream)</u>
   Total flow: FEU (m³/hr)
   Mean concentration of controlled substance: CE (mg/m³)
	Flow: FPD (m³/hr)
	Permitted concentration of controlled substance:
	n (mg/m³)
		Total flow: FRU + FEU + FPD (m³/hr)
		
		Maximum desirable downstream river concentration of controlled substance: RQS (mg/m³)

M_1 = total amount of controlled substance in river upstream of proposed discharge
 	
   = (FRU x CRU) + (FEU x CE)
	M_2 = amount of controlled substance in proposed discharge (mg/hr)
	
	   = FPD x n
		M_3 = total amount of controlled substance in river downstream of proposed discharge (mg/hr)
		
		   = (FRU + FEU + FPD) RQS

By mass balance: $M_1 + M_2 = M_3$

$\therefore$ (FRU x CRU) + (FEU x CE) + FPD x n = (FRU + FEU + FPD) RQS

n, maximum concentration permitted in discharge =

$$\frac{(FRU + FEU + FPD)\ RQS - (FRU \times CRU) - (FEU \times CE)}{FPD}$$

* These data should be based on representative dry weather flow conditions. The Anglian Water Authority publication recommended use of 1973 mean flow conditions.

Appendix 2.3(g)   Reference Summary RS 7 - Discharge Consents and Compliance - The NRA's Approach to Control of Discharge to Water

Purpose and Scope

The purpose of the document is to provide information for dischargers and the public on the National Rivers Authority's (NRA) approach to the control of discharges to water. It provides an overview of the evolving legal framework within which the NRA exercises its discharge control powers. It describes the consent setting process and gives information on and results of consent monitoring and enforcement.

(The role of the former NRA is now part of the remit of the Environment Agency but this publication is still valid.)

Main Contents

The report covers:

- The principles of discharge control policy.
- The legal framework and the NRA's operating practices.
- Developments in discharge consenting.
- Discharge consents, compliance and enforcement statistics for 1990 - 92.

It provides a wide range of information about discharges and consent procedures. It has limited information for assessing the significance of discharges, but does cover some of the technical considerations that have to be considered when applying for a consent to discharge.

Features

Types of Discharges

Discharges to controlled waters fall into 3 main categories, namely isolated pollution incidents (e.g. accidental spills), diffuse pollution (e.g. agricultural run-off) and point source discharges (e.g. from a fixed pipe).

Discharge consents are only used with point source discharges. Diffuse and accidental pollution are controlled using other measures such as codes of practice for product use and physical pollution prevention measures, e.g. bunding of storage tanks, fire water containment lagoons, etc.

The characteristics of point source discharges that determine their environmental impact are:

- Load of substance/substances in the discharge.
- Dilution available in the receiving waters.
- Position of the discharge - geographically and in terms of other discharges.
- Nature of the released substances (with respect to aquatic toxicity, bio-accumulation potential, persistence, biodegradability, solubility and visibility).

The document discusses a number of different types of discharge (sewage, heavy and light industry, food industry and site drainage) and the related potentially polluting substances associated with them.

Legal Basis for Controlling Discharges

The document reviews the historical development of water pollution control legislation, and highlights significant sections of current regulations.

Consent Setting Procedure

Figure A10 shows the steps involved in the consent setting procedure. For most discharges the main criterion that NRA uses to consider a consent application is the need to meet the water quality objectives and appropriate quality standards for the proposed receiving waters. The NRA sets conditions in the consent that will ensure that the desired river water quality is protected.

The NRA uses several techniques to determine calculate the appropriate numerical limits in the consent conditions. The most common methods they use are the combined distribution (CD) methods which are based on a mass balance equation. More complex computer models of transport and degradation are also used, particularly for estuaries and coastal waters and they are making increasing use of river catchment modelling to assess the cumulative impact of a number of effluent discharges.

The simplest form of the mass balance equation is:

$$T = \left(\frac{FC + fc}{F + f} \right)$$

where T is the concentration of the substance downstream of the discharge, F is the river flow upstream of the discharge, C is the concentration of substance upstream of the discharge, f is the flow of the discharge and c is the concentration of substance in the discharge.

The consent procedure also involves public consultation at different phases; charges are levied on the applicant; details of the proposed discharge are recorded in a public register and there is a system for appealing against any decisions made by the NRA.

Compliance Assessment and enforcement

A discharge complies when it fully conforms with the limits set in the consent, as measured by the NRA's audit monitoring programme. Compliance to numerical conditions is assessed through monitoring of pollutant levels both in the discharge and in the receiving waters, the latter to assess if the water quality objectives are being met. Discharge consent limits are set as either:

- absolute limits - to be complied with at all times, or
- percentile limits - where compliance is required for a percentage, e.g. 95%, of the total time.

A consent may also specify non-numerical conditions (e.g. keeping records) and failure to comply with these conditions would also be a breach of the consent.

The NRA monitors effluents and river water regularly to check compliance with discharge consent conditions. When a discharge is found to be outside the specified limits the NRA will take appropriate enforcement action, depending on the circumstances that have caused the non-compliance and the severity of any harmful effects in the receiving water. Enforcement actions range from a warning with encouragement to the operator to correct weaknesses in his control systems or make other changes to reduce the risk of future non-compliance, to prosecution.

Charging Systems

Existing legislation gives the NRA the power to recover the costs of issuing consents and monitoring compliance against them. There is a one-off charge for an application and an on-going annual charge based on the volume and content of the discharge and the characteristics of the receiving waters. Charges are reviewed annually.

Potential Changes to the Consent and Compliance Procedures

The report discusses possible changes to the consent system following the recommendations made in "The Kinnersley Report - Discharge Consent and Compliance Policy: A Blueprint for the Future". The Urban Waste Water Treatment Directive will lead to changes in the consent system for sewage treatment works and the Environment Agency is currently investigating the feasibility of toxicity assessment as a basis for regulating discharges.

Advantages

- Provides general overview of the procedure for obtaining consents.
- Details different types of consents and their specific conditions.
- Provides a basic overview of legislative requirements for dischargers.

Limitations

- Limited information on how to assess if the discharge is acceptable.
- No indication of format of water quality objectives.
- No specific guidance on how to use water quality objectives in assessing the acceptability of a discharge.

Figure A10 Consent Setting Procedure

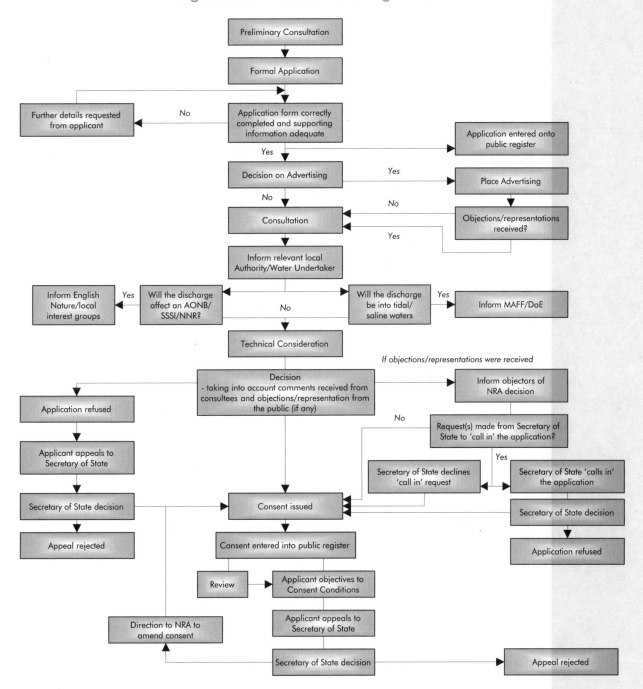

Related Information

The Kinnersley Report - *Discharge Consent and Compliance Policy: A Blueprint for the Future* (NRA: Water Quality Series No 1, July 1990) details recommendations made regarding amending the consents and compliance systems.

Howarth W., (1988), *Water Pollution Law* gives a good overview of water legislation.

Proposals for Statutory Water Quality Objectives, NRA, 1991, discusses the setting of water quality objectives.

Appendix 2.3(h) Reference Summary RS8 - Dispersion in Estuaries and Coastal Waters

Purpose and Scope

To review of the basic mechanisms which disperse dissolved substances in tidal waters and describe how these processes are expressed in dilution models.

Main Contents

- Introduction
- Fluid dynamics - homogeneous flow
- Fluid dynamics - stratified flow
- Turbulent diffusion
- Shear dispersion
- Modelling dispersion
- Methodology for measurement and observation
- Studies of well mixed systems
- Studies of stratified systems
- Studies of partially stratified systems

Useful Features

Formula for buoyant rise dilution (Section 6.2)

A typical family of dilution curves were those established by Abraham (1963) on the basis of experiments with jets in tanks of still water. These curves relate the minimum dilution achieved in a rising jet to the water depth, the diameter of the exit orifice and the 'jet Froude number' F_i of the flow. The Froude number is related to the instantaneous density of the jet, r_i, and the ambient water density, r_a, at jet exit velocity, u, by the expression,

$$F_j = \frac{u}{(g'd_j)^{0.5}}$$

where $g' = g\,(\rho_a\text{-}\rho_i)/\rho_a$ and d_i is the diameter of the jet. A useful formula for the dilution D_0 resulting from entrainment which gives a similar result to Abraham's dilution curves is

$$D_0 = 0.54F_j(\frac{0.38h}{d_jF_j} + 0.66)^{5/3}$$

where h is the total water depth.

Formula for dilution along axis of a waste plume (Section 7.2.2)

The minimum dilution D on the plume axis after dispersing over a time t (secs) is given by

$$D = \frac{1}{Q_v}[\pi u_0(\sigma_{y0}^2 + 2K_yt)^{\frac{1}{2}}(\sigma_{z0}^2 + 2K_zt)^{\frac{1}{2}}]$$

where Q_v is the volume discharge rate (m³ s⁻¹) of effluent and u_0 is the flow velocity (m s⁻¹) past the outfall.

As an example, consider a discharge which is diluted 30 times at the buoyant rise stage so that the field over the outfall has a width = 8.0 m and depth = 0.46 m; the corresponding standard deviations s_{y0}, s_{z0} are one quarter and one half of these two values respectively (i.e. 2.0 m and 0.23 m). For typical mixing coefficients $K_y = 0.025$ m² s⁻¹ and $K_z = 0.0023$ m² s⁻¹, after 10 minutes of spreading in a steady current u_0,

$$D \approx 30.7\frac{u_0}{Q_c}$$

This is only an approximate formula and only really applies to an effluent which has undergone 30 times dilution at the initial entrainment stage. However, the magnitude of D is probably typical of the minimum dilution in an effluent plume which has not mixed down to the seabed.

<u>Allowance for a boundary (Section 6.3.2)</u>

Modification of the plume formula to allow for the effect of the seabed in restricting dilution.

Advantages

- Gives minimum dilution under relatively unfavourable mixing conditions and should be acceptable to Environment Agency as a rough screen.
- Observed values for mixing coefficients Ky, Kz for U.K. coastal waters are tabulated in the book.

Limitations

- No account is taken of tidal variations or wind.
- Does not provide indication of tidal average concentration.

Related Information

Bowden K. F., (1983) *Physical Oceanography for Coastal Waters*, Ellis Horwood, Chichester.

Dyer K. R., (1997) *Estuaries: A Physical Introduction* (Second Edition). John Wiley and Sons, New York, 465 pp.

Fischer H.B., List E.J., Koh R.C.Y., Imberger J. and Brooks N.H. (1979), *Mixing in Inland and Coastal Waters*, Academic Press, New York.

Officer C.B., (1976) *Physical Oceanography of Estuaries (and associated Coastal Waters)* John Wiley and Sons, New York 465 pp.

Williams B.L. (Ed.) (1985), *Ocean Outfall Handbook*. Water and Soil Miscellaneous Publication No. 76, Wellington, New Zealand.

Appendix 2.3 (j) Reference Summary RS9 - A Procedure to Include Deposition in the Model for Short and Medium Range Atmospheric Dispersion of Radionuclides (Report NRPB-R122)

Purpose and Scope

This report is a sequel to the report on atmospheric dispersion of emissions containing radioactive substances, described in RS3 - Appendix 2.3(c). It describes a method for extending the original model to include dry and wet deposition. As with RS3, although the title and text refer to the dispersion of radio-active substances, the model and its treatment of deposition are valid for any emissions of gases or fine particles.

Contents

The main contents of the report are:

- a summary of the original model for short and medium range dispersion
- a "source-depletion" model to represent dry deposition with tabulated results showing plume depletion for a range of stability categories and stack heights
- a wet deposition model to estimate additional deposition due to washout by rainfall

Features

The dispersion model described in RS3 is based on the simplifying assumption that a dispersing plume is fully reflected when it reaches the ground and there is no loss of material from the plume. In reality material will be lost from a plume in contact with the ground by a variety of mechanisms, including impaction and chemical reaction with vegetation. Collectively these processes are called "dry deposition". Material can also be removed from a dispersing plume by being washed out by rainfall. This process is called "wet deposition".

For dry deposition this report recommends a "source depletion model" to represent the removal of material from the plume by deposition on the ground. This type of model assumes that the material remaining in the plume retains a Gaussian distribution pattern in both the vertical and horizontal planes. Two tables of results show the fraction of material remaining in a plume for a range of effective release heights and Pasquill stability categories; one set of results applies to a short release and the other to a continuous release. One example is shown in Figure A11 which shows the fraction of material remaining in the plume at various distance from a continuous release from a 20m stack under each Pasquill category.

Dry deposition rate is calculated using the concept of deposition velocity, defined as the ratio of substance deposited per unit area in unit time to the concentration of the substance in the air at ground level. The relevant concentration is that calculated by the model described above and a deposition velocity of 10^{-2} m s^{-1} is suggested. A later report (NRPB-R157, 1983) from the same authors suggested a deposition velocity range of 10^{-2} to 3×10^{-2} m s^{-1} as appropriate for 10μm particles.

When it is raining both wet and dry deposition mechanisms will occur so the total rate of deposition will be the sum of both processes. The report gives a graph showing the fraction of material remaining in a plume subject to wet deposition under Pasquill stability category D conditions for a range of washout coefficients (fraction of material removed from the plume by rainfall in unit time.) For estimating purposes the report suggests assuming that rainfall only occurs under category D conditions and for 10% of the time.

Figure A 11 The fraction of material remaining in the plume due to dry deposition for a continuous release and a deposition velocity of 10^{-2} m s^{-1} for each Pasquill category

Stack height: 30m

Pasquill Category	Wind speed at stack ht. m. s^{-1}	Fraction left in plume at distance indicated					
		100m	200m	500m	1000m	2000m	5000m
A	1.32	0.997	0.986	0.962	0.941	0.919	0.886
B	2.65	1.00	0.995	0.979	0.960	0.939	0.904
C	6.62	1.00	0.999	0.992	0.983	0.970	0.949
D	6.62	1.00	1.00	0.995	0.983	0.965	0.933
E	3.97	1.00	1.00	0.997	0.979	0.941	0.864
F	2.65	1.00	1.00	1.00	0.991	0.949	0.791
G	1.32	1.00	1.00	1.00	1.00	0.990	0.798

The amount of material deposited along the path of the plume can be calculated from these figures. Under category D conditions, 0.5% of the material released is deposited between 200m and 500m; a further 1.2 % is deposited between 500m and 1000m; a further 1.8% between 1000m and 2000m and a further 3.2% between 2000m and 5000m.

The maximum rate of deposition is somewhere between 500m and 1000m. Graphical interpolation can be used to give a more precise estimate of the area where maximum deposition is likely.

A more conservative estimate of the maximum dry deposition rate, which does not allow for any deposition and depletion from the plume upwind of the point of maximum ground level concentration in air, can be obtained by multiplying the maximum ground level concentration, as determined using RS3, by 10^{-2} m s^{-1}. This very simple approach is useful as an initial screen of deposition rates to identify releases that are trivial in respect of deposition rates.

Appendix 2.3(k) List of additional references dealing with the dispersion of releases into the environment

Author/Publisher	Title	Year
References for Air		
Environmental Analysis Co-operative, HMSO	Released Substances and their Dispersion in the Environment	1996
Department of the Environment, HMSO	The National Air Quality Strategy	1996
+Cheremisinoff P. N. and Young R. A., Marcel Dekker	Air Pollution Control and Design Handbook	1977
Harrison R. M. published by The Royal Socisty of Chemistry, 3rd edition	Pollution: Causes, Effects and Control	1993
Hall D. J. and Kukadia V., Warren Spring Laboratory LR 929	Background to the new HMIP Guidelines on Discharge Stack Heights for Polluting Emissions	1993
Prepared by the Environment Agency, Department of Environment and DNV	Guidance for Estimating the Air Quality Impact of Stationary Sources	1998
References for Odour		
Hall and Kukadia	Approaches to the Calculation of Discharge Stacks for Odour Control	1994
References to Water		
Bowden K. F., Ellis Horwood, Chichester	Physical Oceanography for Coastal Waters	1983
Dyer K. R., John Wiley and Sons, New York	Estuaries: A Physical Introduction (2nd Edition)	1997
Fischer H. B., List E. J., Koh R. C. Y., Imberger J. and Brooks N. H., Academic Press, New York	Mixing in Inland and Coastal Waters	1979
Howarth W.	Water Pollution Law	1988
Officer C. B., John Wiley and Sons, New York	Physical Oceanography of Estuaries (and associated Coastal Waters)	1976
Williams B. L. Ed.), Wellington, New Zealand	Ocean Outfall Handbook, Water and Soil Miscellaneous Publication No. 76	1985

Appendix 2.3(I) Models used in Air and Water Dispersion Modelling

Tables 1 and 2 are lists of models that are available for the more detailed modelling of dispersion that may be necessary for assessing *significant* releases into air and water. These lists are not exhaustive. The Internet is now a further source of information which can be used for identifying other models.

Table 1 Air Dispersion Models

Model	Name and Origin	Key features*
ADMS ● Screening ● Standard ● Urban	Atmospheric dispersion Modelling System (CERC)	● Long-term, short term and percentile options ● Volume, area, line, point, sources ● Multiple sources ● Complex terrain ● Buildings effects ● Graphical information system ● Deposition
ISC	Industry Source Complex (US EPA/Trinity Consultants)	● Pasquill stability classes ● Long-term and short-term and percentile ● Volume, area, line, point sources ● Canyon buildings model ● Multiple sources ● Simple terrain ● Buildings effects ● "Gravitational settling" of large particles
AERMOD	(US EPA)	● Recently developed ● Long-term and short-term and percentiles ● Built in mcontour plotting ● Multiple sources ● Graphical information system ● Deposition ● Complex terrain ● Buildings effects
R91	(Tessella for HMIP/CERC)	● Pasquill stability classes ● Long-term and short-term ● DOS based ● Output not user friendly

* Features might vary with different versions.

Table 2 List if Models for Water Dispersion

Model	Name and Origin	Key Features*
CORMIX	Cornell Mixing Zone Model	● Routine discharge studies ● Single/multiple port releases ● International recognition
SWMM	Storm Water Management Model	● Urban run-off model ● Hydrology and quality of pollutant influxes into sewer systems and rivers ● Accidental releases
SIMCAT	Simulation of Catchment	● Calculates quality of river water in catchment area ● Used for discharge consents
PRAIRIE	Pollution Risk from Accidental Influxes of rivers and setuaries	● Risk assessment methodology
MIKE		● Analysis, planning and management of water resources

* Features might vary with different versions.

APPENDICES FOR CHAPTER 3

Environmental Monitoring and Ambient Quality Data

Contents

Appendix 3.4 (a) Computer simulation of AC, PC and PEC - to illustrate the relation between annual average and high percentile values of concentrations of a substance in air

The hourly means of ambient and process concentrations of a pollutant are plotted on the two charts in Figure A-12. The values of annual mean, 100th and 90th percentiles are also indicated.   The differences between the two sets of data are apparent and it is clear that the two charts vary independently.

The two charts in Figure A-13 show the AC and the PC added together on an hour by hour basis to give the true hourly mean PECs over a year.   This detailed data would not be available in reality because the AC data is historic from actual air quality monitoring while the PC, in practice, would be the predictions from a dispersion model. We are using a computer simulation of both sets of data here to show, in the left hand chart, that the true 100th percentile PEC (from all hourly mean PECs over a year), is much lower than the 100th percentile produced by the method of adding 100th percentile AC and 100th percentile PC. In this case, the latter value exceeds the EQC.

Alternative simpler methods of making a reasonable estimate of the maximum PEC are as follows:

1. The 90th percentile approach to calculating a PEC is illustrated in the right hand chart in Figure A 13. This uses: ***100th percentile PC + 90th percentile AC.*** It is a less conservative estimate of the PEC and, in this example, is less than the EQC. However, if the stack is tall and the maximum AC and PC are unlikely to coincide, then it can be argued that this would be a more realistic approach and the process might be determined to be acceptable.

2. The PEC calculated using twice the annual average AC is also illustrated in the same chart. This uses: ***2 x annual average AC + 100th percentile PC.*** This gives an estimate of PEC very similar to the above method.

Figure A-12   Example data for Ambient Concentrations and Process Contributions

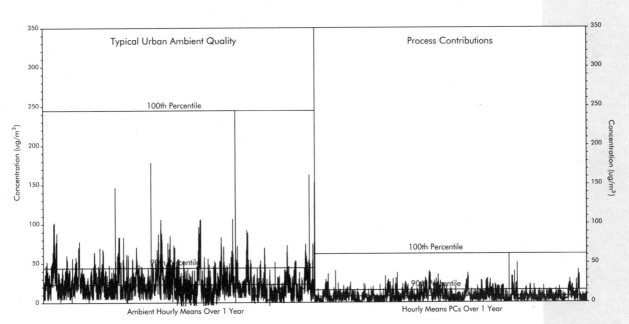

Figure A-13 Examples of Predicted Environmental Concentrations

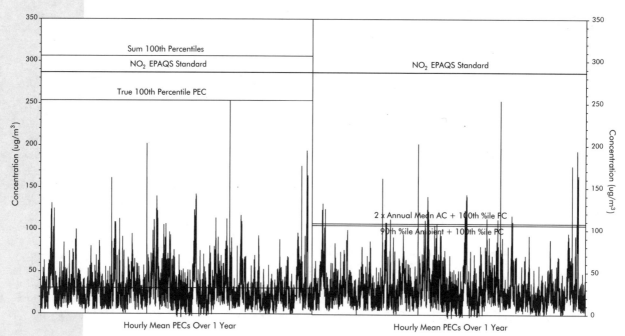

Appendix 3.4 (b) UK air quality monitoring networks

The following notes describe the main features of each network and Figure A.14 provides an overall summary table of all the networks. The table also shows which networks are checking compliance with statutory air quality standards (see Appendix 2.2(a)).

Automatic Networks

The automatic networks have instruments that sample and analyse the ambient air continuously. These measurements are stored at site in a data logging system, which is interrogated automatically every hour by modem to retrieve the results. Data are then processed by computer systems and released as provisional hourly statistics through the data dissemination unit at NETCEN.

Non-Automatic Networks

These cover a variety of pollutants and monitoring techniques. In general air is sampled onto a medium, either into solution or on a filter, over a long averaging time: from daily to quarterly. The sample is removed from the location and the results obtained by analysis of the medium in a laboratory.

The NO_2 Diffusion Tube Network uses monthly diffusion tubes and has been in existence since 1993.

The Smoke and Sulphur Dioxide Network provide daily samples from acidified H_2O_2 bubblers and smoke filters. The H_2O_2 is analysed by titration to determine SO_2 and the filters are analysed by reflectance to determine smoke. This network has been in operation for over 30 years.

Samples in the Multi-Element (Cd, Cr, Cu, Fe, Mn, Ni, Pb and Zn) and Lead Networks are collected on filters and analysed by ionised current plasma analysis (ICP-AES), or Atomic Absorption Spectroscopy. The rural sites started monitoring in 1972 and urban and industrial sites after 1976.

The Acid Deposition Network measures the composition of precipitation (rain, snow, mist) at 32 sites across the UK. Samples are analysed for conductivity, pH, cations (NH_4^+, Na^+, K^+, Ca^{2+}, Mg^{2+}) and anions (NO_3^-, Cl^-, SO_4^{2-} and PO_4^{3-}). Daily SO_2 and particulate sulphate are also measured at a subset of sites.

Weekly SO_2 is measured in the Rural SO_2 Monitoring Network using a similar technique to the Smoke and SO_2 network, i.e. an H_2O_2 bubbler. However, the analysis is by ion chromatography which avoids the problem of interference by other acidic gases.

Toxic organic micropollutants (TOMPS) are measured at 3 urban background sites and 3 rural sites monitoring a large range of dioxins and PAH's (polyaromatic hydrocarbons).

Figure A.-14   UK Monitoring Networks at 1st September 1997

(Private) Network	Urban	Hydrocarbon	Rural	Diffusion Tube	Smoke /SO₂	Lead + Multi-Element	Acid Deposition	Rural SO₂	TOMPS[4]
Pollutants	O^3 NO_X SO_2 CO PM_{10}	25 Species	O_3 NO_X SO_2	NO_2	Smoke/ SO_2	Pb Metals	Anions and Cations NO_2 SO_4	SO2	PAH's PCB's Dioxins
Site Number	75[2]	12[3]	19[1]	1190	222	28	32	37	4
Measurement Technique	A	A	A	PS	AS	AS	AS, PS	AS	AS
Function	S	N	S	N	S	S	N	N	N

A = Automatic   AS = Active Sampler   PS = Passive Sampler   S = Statutory   N = Non Statutory

[1] Includes one site operated by PowerGen and four affiliate sites.
[2] Includes thirty-nine affiliate sites.
[3] Hydrocarbon monitoring at Southampton, Middlesbrough, Birmingham East and London Eltham is co-located with an urban monitoring network site. Hydrocarbon monitoring at Harwell is co-located with a rural monitoring network site.
[4] Toxic Organic Micropollutants.

Appendix 3.5   Fate of substances in soil

The physical and chemical properties of soils vary so widely from one place to another that it is not possible to make reliable generalised predictions about the fate of a particular substance in soil. The problem is further complicated by the variety of physical and chemical processes that may contribute to the degradation of a substance in soil. These include dissolution and leaching, adsorption, partitioning into soil particles, reaction with soil matter, diffusion, biological degradation and volatilisation.

The only general conclusions that can be drawn are qualitative. Sandy soil with large particles and pores tend to be well drained and tend not to bind contaminants. Clayey soils tend to be poorly drained and to bind contaminants.

Measured data on the fate of substances in soil is mostly limited to laboratory studies under controlled conditions using standard soils. These methods produce results which are useful for comparing the relative behaviour of substances but may be orders of magnitude away from the behaviour of a substance in a real situation.

Degradation processes in soil can be modelled using the physical and chemical characteristics of a substance, such as partition coefficients, solubility, vapour pressure and dissociation constant, but the models all involve assumptions and approximations.

The rate at which a substance degrades in soil is normally expressed as its "half-life", being the time for 50% of the substance to degrade to unspecified products. Another measure which is often confused with half-life is the time for 50% of the substance to disappear from the soil. The word "disappear" in this context means that the substance cannot be recovered from the soil. Thus it include other processes, such as volatilisation and irreversible binding onto soil particles, as well as chemical decomposition. The 50% disappearance value is referred to as Dt_{50}.

In spite of all the difficulties, values of half-life or Dt_{50} have been published for organic chemicals in soil. The table in Figure A15 gives a selection of values from the references quoted below. The values are shown here to give an idea of the range of values from different sources and the order of magnitude of the values for various types of organic compounds.

It is extremely unlikely that planned releases of organic compounds from an IPC process would lead to significant deposition onto land and the need to take account of half-lives in soil. However, if your assessment of significance indicated that there may be a significant impact it would be advisable to discuss the matter with the Environment Agency before firming up on the design of your process.

Figure A 15   Half-life and Dt_{50} values of some substances in soil

Substance	Quoted half-life	Quoted Dt_{50}
Benzene	5 - 16 days	< 2 days
Toluene	4 - 22 days	< 2 days
Ethyl benzene	3 - 10 days	
Xylenes	7 - 28 days	2.2 days
Napthalene	2.1 days	12 - 125 days
Fluorene	32 - 60 days	
Phenanthrene	16 - 200 days	2.5 - 26 days
Anthracene	50 - 460 days	3.3 - 175 days
Pyrene	0.5 - 5.2 days	3 - 35 days
Benz(a)pyrene	57 - 330 days	
Phenol	2 - 5 days	
Chlorophenols	1 - 20 days	
Chloroform	20 days	
Trichloroethylene	no degradation after 25 weeks	

Substance	Quoted half-life	Quoted Dt$_{50}$
Pyridine	66 - 170 days	
Chlorobenzene	2 - 5 months	2.1 days
Dichlorobenzenes	1 - 6 months	
Trichlorobenzenes	1 - 6 months	
Hexachlorobenzenes	2.5 - 5.7 years	
Tetrachloro-dibenzo-p-dioxin	1.1 - 1.6 years or 10 - 12 years	~ 10 years
Aldrin	20 - 100 days	
Atrazine	330 - 385 days	
Chlordane	3.3 years	
Dieldrin	> 7 years	
Dichlorvos	7 days	
Endrin	~ 14 years	
Heptachlor	0.4 - 0.8 years	

This selection of values is taken from the following sources:

Mackay, D., Shiu, W.Y., and Ma, K.C., (1992) - *Illustrated Handbook of Physical-Chemical Properties and Environmental Fate data for Organic Chemicals*, Vols. 1 & 2, Lewis Publishers, Boca Raton, Florida, USA, and

Howard, P.H., (1989) - *Handbook of Environmental Fate and Exposure Data for Organic Chemicals,* Vol. 1: Large Production and Priority Pollutants. Lewis Publishers, Boca Raton, USA.

INDEX